Other Books by John Malcolm Brinnin

POETRY

The Garden is Political

The Lincoln Lyrics

No Arch, No Triumph

The Sorrows of Cold Stone

The Selected Poems of John Malcolm Brinnin

Skin Diving in the Virgins

BIOGRAPHY

Dylan Thomas in America

The Third Rose: Gertrude Stein and Her World

Sextet: T.S. Eliot & Truman Capote & Others

HISTORY

The Sway of the Grand Saloon

CRITICISM

Emily Dickinson, *a selection of poems*

Casebook on Dylan Thomas, *a collection of essays*

William Carlos Williams, *a critical study*

Selected Plays of Gertrude Stein

ANTHOLOGIES

Modern Poetry: American and British
  (*with Kimon Friar*)

The Modern Poets: An American-British Anthology
  (*with Bill Read*)

FOR CHILDREN

Arthur, The Dolphin Who Didn't See Venice

JOHN MALCOLM BRINNIN

BEAU VOYAGE
LIFE ABOARD THE LAST GREAT SHIPS

Conceived, compiled, and designed by

Michel Mohrt and Guy Feinstein

DORSET PRESS

New York

*Special thanks are due to John Hollis of Whitman, Massachusetts,
for his good counsel and tracing of errors.*

Grateful acknowledgment is made to the museum curators and navigation companies who assisted in the collection of the photographs, often hitherto unpublished, contained in this book, and especially:

Mr. P. de Tauligan and Mr. R. Bouvard of the Compagnie Générale Transatlantique; Mr. Louis Gacon of the Compagnie des Mesageries Maritimes; Mr. Stephen Rabson, P & O line, London; Miss June E. Foster, Union Castle Line, London; Mme. J. Rymarezyk, Compagnie des Chargeurs Réunis; Mr. Peter Grout, The British Council, Paris; Mr. Finck, HAPAG Lloyd, Hamburg; Mrs. E. Stielow, Preussicher Kulturbesitz, Berlin; Mr. Michael Cook, M.A., of the University of Liverpool; Mr. Richard J. Huyda, chief curator of the Public Archives, Ottawa, Canada; Mme. Raymonde Litalien, French representative of the Canadian Public Archives; Baron Limnander de Nieuwenhove, former purser of the Compagnie Générale Transatlantique; Mme. Dufy; Mr. Robert Rook; and Mr. J.-C. Tronquez.

Text copyright © 1981 by John Malcolm Brinnin.

Illustrations first published in France as *Paquebots: Le temps des traversées,*
1980, copyright © 1980 by Editions Maritimes et d'Outre Mer.

Library of Congress Cataloging in Publication Data
Brinnin, John Malcolm, 1916–   Beau voyage.
Illustrations originally published in: Paquebots / Michel Mohrt.
1. Ocean travel. 2. Ocean liners. I. Mohrt, Michel. Paquebots. II. Title.
G550.B74   910.4′5   81-5451   AACR2

This edition published by Dorset Press,
a division of Marboro Books Corporation,
by arrangement with Editions Jean Claude Lattès.
1987 Dorset Press

ISBN 0-88029-140-0

Translations from the French by Richard Miller

7-30-04
Printed and bound in Yugoslavia
M 9 8 7 6 5 4 3 2 1

CONTENTS

A SHIP BUFF

In Twickenham, Middlesex, England, on the morning of June 7, 1966, the author of these notes was on his hands and knees in the company of two men in white laboratory coats who were also on their hands and knees. In front of us, a large teakettle sat on a hotplate. Around us, spread across the floor like toys under a Christmas tree, were a dozen little cylinders, three or four inches in length, each of a different shape and open at both ends.

"Let's try that one again," said the man beside me, and pointed to a cylinder from which two flat metal protuberances extended like the ears of a running dog. As I handed it over, he spoke to his companion. "Turn up the heat—let's see how it goes full steam."

Connecting the cylinder to the kettle, he then reached over and turned on an electric fan. As steam began to whistle, wind from the fan blew on it to create a trail of vapor five or six feet long. "Not bad," said the man. "Those ears, I like the way they ride. Now let's have a go at the one with the sampan top."

What we were doing was observing the angles of wind flow on little prototype funnels, one of which would be chosen for a ship then known only as "Q 4." Five years later, the most curiously shaped one of them all—a thin black stack with white cladding on its sides and a curving wind scoop at its base—would be visible a thousandfold larger when, for the first time, the *Queen Elizabeth 2* came into New York Harbor.

What had brought me there was curiosity, a hunger to know from the inside what all my life I'd known about ships only from the outside. Two years earlier the Cunard Line, having scrapped plans to build a gigantic successor to the *Queen Mary* and *Queen Elizabeth*, had decided to go ahead with a ship more in tune with the times, a luxury liner that would offer summer crossings of the Atlantic and winter cruises of so wide a range that she would have to be versatile enough to sail under the bridge at Bilbao or squeeze through the Panama Canal. When I'd learned of this and guessed that she would be the last great passenger ship ever to be built, I was determined to watch her grow; and so I did, from the day when she was no more than a little red platform of steel to the day when, towering like a battlement of Piranesi proportions, she moved one inch, two inches, then slid on tons of tallow into the river Clyde.

In the time between, I had come to know her designers and shipwrights, the decorators who made her one of the most surprising artifacts of British imagination, and the managers who would systematically trash and mistreat her to the point where she became an embarrassment to those who conceived and crafted her and, to those who sailed in her, the saddest relict of an era she might have reprieved and prolonged.

How some individuals come to be obsessed with ships and the lore of the sea when so many other phenomena are available to their attention remains a mystery. Yet, like members of some secret society or outlaw cabal, we recognize one another by the whisper of a statistic, or the hint of a maritime accident, and take for granted a fund of knowledge the man in the street finds impenetrable or redundant.

Temperamentally, I tend to resist the claims of geneticists and genealogists that predisposition makes this or that role in life inevitable. Too many people skip the genetic link, or drop from the genealogical branch, to allow me to accept destiny as an explanation for the careers of those who don't. Yet, in my case, evidences of a predisposition on both scores are difficult to ignore. My maternal ancestors were seafarers sailing schooners on coastal routes between Nova Scotia and Labrador, sometimes ranging as far south as St. Kitts and what used to be called "the Barbadoes." A distant great-uncle of mine was Chief Engineer on one of the early Cunarders, and, as it happened, I was born within walking distance of the home of Samuel Cunard himself. Brought up in the Midwest, I'd spend every summer in Nova Scotia, where my playmates just across the street were the son and daughter of the designer of the legendary schooner *Bluenose*; and where the houses of my relatives were small museums of nautical artifacts collected by family members who became wireless operators on ships, or supercargoes, or, in one case, a First Mate always, it seemed, "up Hudson Bay."

The first word I ever spoke, my parents told me, was an effort to pronounce *Olympic*, the name of the sister ship of the *Titanic*, which in the course of World War I came regularly to Halifax as a troopship. My first recorded utterance occurred while I was being pushed in a pram along one of the harborside slopes from which could be seen the traffic of oceangoing ships entering or leaving the great backwater of Bedford Basin; and this effort was rewarded by so much amused attention that, for months on end, every ship in the harbor was "limpic." When I was old enough to walk, my mother took me by the hand to see the cemetery that stands at the corner of Barrington Street and the street on which I was born, Spring Garden Road. Among old stones was a comparatively new row of crosses. These, I was told, were the grave markers of men and women pulled from the water days after the *Titanic* had disappeared. When I was eleven or twelve, another relative of mine became skipper of the ferryboat plying the harbor between Halifax and Dartmouth. In the long afternoons I'd spend on its decks, he'd now and then allow me into the pilothouse and let me take the wheel. And on days when something as astounding as the *Berengaria* was in port, I'd make my way to her dock just to hang around in the presence of a phenomenon that fascinated me in ways it would take a lifetime to understand. Summer after summer, the only calendar I paid attention to was an invisible one on which the days of the week and the time of the month were established by the arrivals and departures of ships I knew.

Years later, when I'd begun to write poetry and was properly moony and given to solitude in chequered shades, another great ship provided the most beautiful sight I had until then seen. With a book under my arm, I had wandered into the park at Point Pleasant, where, on a green knoll or a scarp of granite, I'd stop now and then to read, or make a note, or say aloud a stanza I had memorized. Communing only with myself, I looked up at one point and there, sliding through a stand of pine trees and so close I felt I could reach out and touch her, was the enormous *Britannic*, her funnels smoking, her black bow silently insinuating itself through the sun-shot forest. Unaware, I had come to the edge of a bluff on the harbor, along which the ship continued to her berth at the Ocean Terminals.

Years before I ever thought of traveling on a ship, I could, if asked, say where almost any one of them working the North Atlantic was, and where she was going. But I had actually seen only those that came to Halifax. To learn what those I'd not seen looked like inside and out, I resorted to strategy, the first instance of which succeeded only at the cost of mortification. I must have been nine or ten when I asked my mother to take me to one of the shipping offices that served as a general agency. There, a broad table spread with brochures for a score of steamship lines was, to my eyes, a smorgasbord of which I would never get enough. As I selected dozens of them indiscriminately, at the same time curbing my greed so that I might have an excuse to come back for more, the clerk in charge asked me if he might be of assistance.

"I want to go to Europe," I told him.

Staring at my bundle of thirty or forty brochures, he asked, "In what class do you intend to travel?"

What *class*?! The idea of such a thing on the ocean had never crossed my mind. Exposed for the fraud I was, I braved him out. "I'll have to think about it," I said, and clutched the brochures like money.

The clerk winked at my mother. "Well," he said, "it's always nice to know about all classes before you make up your mind, isn't it?"

My first voyage was made on the *Queen Mary* when, barely a month in service, she sailed from New York. No one knew then that, against all the statistics, measurements, and gaga descriptions of luxury for which she was responsible, she would throughout her time prevail as a ship and not as a grand hotel afloat. Or that, like legendary women, she was more than the sum of her parts, the details of her history, or all that could be said for or against her. A presence as palpable and visible as she was ultimately unaccountable: The *Queen Mary* would stand for "soul" in the regard of seamen, and with "class" in the affection of those travelers who could discriminate between the obvious and the apt.

But since legends are projections and can be only minimally tied to the vulgarity of fact, they remain impervious to judgment and scrutiny, not excepting mine. We first met in 1936. I was a teenager; she was about to make her second eastward voyage. But I already knew her from the extraordinary publicity attending her first arrival in New York, when she had sailed up the Hudson to the kind of ovation previously reserved for national heroes like General Pershing and Charles Lindbergh. More specifically, I knew her from long perusals of the cross-section chart of her interior with which the Cunard Line had provided travel bureaus. I had got hold of one of these from an obliging agent and, long before sailing day, was thoroughly familiar with all the corridors and companionways I might take when I closed the door of my Third Class cabin, and to what they would lead.

Embarking on a hot July morning, I was surprised by nothing but actuality: the curving vastness of her open decks, the cathedral height and hush of her main lounge, the baronial grandeur of her smoking room, none of which I was to see again for days. A Third Class passenger in a cabin containing four bunks and no bath, I was confined to the forward part of the ship next to the crew's quarters and below the First Class observation lounge with its broad windows looking out upon the foredeck and the plunging prow. But I found this confinement nothing to chafe about. Passengers in Third had a lounge of ample size and pleasant appointment, a dining room that at first glance seemed to be an acre of tablecloth punctuated by carnations in little silver vases, and as many other public rooms, I thought, as anyone might need. What disappointed me was the lack of space to make those "turns about the deck" I'd read about; and a "ship's smell" I'd also read about, in which was combined a vague scent of butter going rancid, or cream going sour, with a sort of underlay of *essence de bilge*. Otherwise entranced by everything, I kept to myself for the first two days, read Lorca and Proust, and did nothing else but watch the sea from a dozen points of vantage inside and out. But even that kind of atavistic reverie, I found, has its term. Third day out, I picked up an acquaintance with a girl from Bryn Mawr, then with the two classmates with whom she was traveling. Both of them were sulking. Having brought evening gowns with them, they had found in Third Class no place or occasion to wear them. Taking on their problem, I suggested we crash First Class around midnight. But how could we cross the border dividing Third from Cabin? one of them asked—not to mention the one dividing Cabin from First.

I told them, in exquisite detail.

This was a mistake. But, as I would understand years later, the response it evoked was in the nature of a lesson I would have to learn. The looks they turned on me were at first surprised, then blank, then slit-eyed. Having posed a simple question, they had to listen to an answer wildly beyond its premises or demands—as if they had asked a casual acquaintance if he didn't think penguins were darling and had then had to endure a lecture on the mating rites of those birds, their feeding customs and bone structures, culminating in a prolonged discourse detailing the comparative incidence of the blue, the jackass, the king, and the emperor and their range of habitat from the Galapagos Islands to Antarctica.

August 17, 1956. The *Nieuw Amsterdam*'s First Officer presides, the sommelier hovers, over a table lately cleared—the author (*foreground*) remembers—of Maine lobster cocktail, turtle soup, filet mignon from the Argentine, *salade de pointes d'asperges*, and baked alaska. In the background, Cardinal Cushing's crucifix dangles over his cherries jubilee and, three decks overhead, the Boston Symphony Orchestra begins to tune up for a midocean concert in the lounge.

Suddenly a bit wary about everything, I thought, they nevertheless decided to give me the chance to prove that I was not the mythomaniac they took me for. Late evening, we were ready to go—I as formal as possible in a blue serge suit from Crowley-Milner's, they in bareshouldered gowns with filmy white skirts. To get above, I told them, we would first have to go below. Down we went, like refugees from *Swan Lake*, into the bowels of the *Queen Mary*, where greasy men monitoring gauges and tending oil-burning furnaces, stunned by the sight of us, politely stood aside to let us pass.

"Gosh!" yelled one of the girls through the din of valves and knocking steampipes. "It's like *The Hairy Ape!*"

Persisting through infernal regions, I led my troupe through boiler rooms 1 and 2, then under the First Class swimming pool into the forward turbogenerator room toward companionways I knew would be there, followed my nose to the elevator I knew would be there, and, presto, gained the bright main deck foyer and went up broad stairs to the tall glass doors opening into the main lounge. As we melted into the crowd around the dance floor, no one thought to congratulate me but myself.

Our landfall was Brittany, a few lights along the shore. Convinced, really, for the first time, that Europe was not a flight of some collective imagination I'd been exposed to but soil I might walk upon, I stayed late and alone on the foredeck, which was lit only by running lights. The night was full of stars, the foremast rocking among them. Unable to sleep or even to think of sleep, I finally went to the writing room and found myself the only one there. On a sheet of paper crested with a little image of the ship I wrote: "Dearest, Lights off the starboard tell me Europe is real and now I think maybe you are real and like England and France and other countries I thought were only postage stamps, you are all there to be explored and known and held, as they are held, most dear."

When I couldn't think of what to say next, I crumpled the sheet, tossed it into a wastebasket, and went to my bunk.

Next morning, as we coasted along the French coast, rain deepened the greenest green I'd ever laid eyes on. In the writing room I took a chair by the window not far from a group of men and women whose random bursts of high spirits suggested that for them the night had not yet ended.

"Get a load of this," said one of the men, and began to read from a crumpled piece of paper he held in his hand. "Dearest, Lights off the starboard tell me Europe is real and now I think you are real," etc. etc.

"You never wrote to *me* like that, Herbie," said a woman in the chair across from his.

"You want that kind of bull, honey," he said, "I'll see that you get it."

Everyone laughed, no one louder than I.

Six weeks later, a nineteen-year-old man of the world, including that *terra incognita* part of it known as the Soviet Union, I boarded the *Aurania* in Le Havre for a crossing that would return me to Detroit via what was then called "the inland route," meaning passage up the St. Lawrence River to Montreal. It was early evening when the second section of the boat train from Paris arrived, and I went on deck to watch the embarkation of latecomers. There I was joined by a middle-aged man smoking a pipe. As we stood at the railing idly observing the Indian-file procession up the open gangplank, we heard behind us the voices of passengers who, exploring the ship, had come onto the deck.

"Mildred, dear," said one of these, "I simply don't know where I've put my Mothersills. Do you know where yours are?"

"If you're going to be seasick, Mother," said another voice, "you're going to be seasick. Why do you have to *think* about it?"

"The young woman's right," said the man beside me. "It's all in the head. People let themselves get seasick before they're halfway up the gangplank. You notice that?"

"It's as though they wanted to have something to talk about," I said. "I came over *this* time on the *Queen Mary* and never felt a twinge."

Cosmopolitan and smug, we both continued to enjoy the point of vantage we had earned. As the last embarking passenger came hurrying aboard, I said good night to my shipmate, lingered awhile on deck to watch the tugboats easing us out into the Channel, then climbed into my low bunk in a bare inside cabin aft.

Seven nights and seven days later, I climbed out of it; but not until the *Aurania* had come to a dead stop in fog surrounding icebergs that remained invisible. In the time between, I had a hundred times alternately lifted my head and fainted back into my own vomit. Later, on land, I could remember intervals when the faces of a doctor and a nurse had hovered over me, or when a steward, handling me like a doll, would attempt to clean my fouled nest. I could remember apples and biscuits that would suddenly appear on my pillow, and I could remember the Tauchnitz edition of Hemingway's *Torrents of Spring* that had dropped from my hands on the night we sailed and, splayed open, lay for days on the floor beneath my bunk. And I could recall moments of utter clarity: the one in which I knew I was going to die, and that terrible one in which I knew that this was not likely. I did not have the deck plans of the *Aurania* in my head as I had those of the *Queen Mary*, yet I knew enough about her to plot an end to my misery. If, in the middle of some night, I could keep from fainting long enough to get up to the first open space, another fainting spell, or even many others, would not matter. Sooner or later, perhaps mercifully assisted by a steward to whom I would give as a tip all the money I had, I'd be over the deck rail and into blessed surcease.

Fourteen years later, I ventured to cross the Atlantic again, on the new *Liberté* of the French Line. This roseate chateau afloat was the old German *Europa*, rehabilitated and transformed. So, as it turned out, was I. On that first brisk day when, loaded with the miraculous new seasickness nostrum Dramamine, I walked her rolling decks and leaned without fear over railings to catch the pitch of her bow and the lift of her stern, "Eureka!" I called into the wind, "Eureka!"

A burst of sea air had opened one of Keats's "charm'd magic casements" to show me a future in which I'd cross the Atlantic as frequently as I once crossed Halifax Harbor and, between these trips, sail on almost everything that rides the water, from Trebizond to Acapulco.

THE BUILDING OF A GREAT SHIP

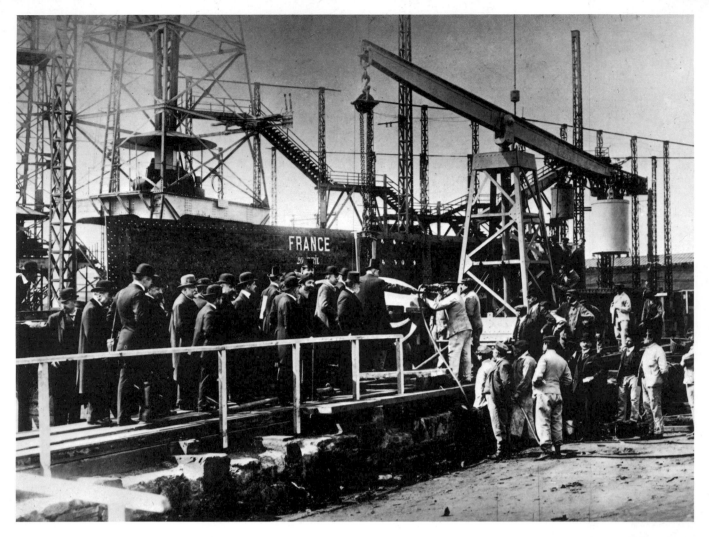

TOP: In the shipyards of Saint-Nazaire, a silk-hatted official rivets the first bolt on the *France*. Launched in 1910, this ship would sail just in time to join the *concours d'élégance* of great new ships that would be abruptly ended by the outbreak of World War I.

BOTTOM: April 1931. Laying the first elements of the hull of the *Normandie*, which, like the *Queen Mary*, was a product of the Great Depression and a supreme emblem of national pride. Both ships were bigger by a third than any ship previously constructed, and both were faster. The last ships to have three

funnels, they were the first to offer passenger accommodations in Third Class equal to those of First Class at the turn of the century.

TOP AND BOTTOM: The hull of the *Normandie* takes shape. Completed in 1935, the French Line flagship was the largest and fastest vessel afloat until the arrival of the *Queen Mary* one year later—setting up a leapfrog rivalry in which they took the Atlantic speed record from one another and during which the *Normandie*'s size was increased by 2,000 tons to give her the edge.

ABOVE: The chains of the *Queen Mary*, each link weighing 180 pounds. Cunard White Star spent four years of research on the shape of the hull and the installation of engines designed to allow the ship to maintain maximum speed in the heaviest of storms. During her shakedown runs, the *Queen Mary* attained a speed of nearly 33 knots, thereby allowing her to make a record westward Atlantic crossing in four days, twenty-seven minutes, and a record eastward voyage in three days, twenty-three hours, fifty-seven minutes, at average speeds of 30.14 and 30.63 knots respectively. Entitled to the Blue Ribbon awarded to the ship making the fastest Atlantic crossing, her owners told the owners of the record-holding *Normandie* to keep it, saying that they did not believe in speed as a point of competition.

OPPOSITE: At the Penhoët yards, before being installed in the *Normandie*, one of four 40,000-horsepower engines which, fed by turbo-alternators, drove the propeller shaft. The power generated by these engines caused excessive vibration when the ship was traveling at high speeds until four-bladed propellers were replaced by three-bladed ones.

OVERLEAF, LEFT: The *Normandie* in the Joubert dock at Saint-Nazaire. In the course of building the ship, the Penhoët yards had to correct an inadequacy by constructing a new sluice dock to serve both as dry dock and lock, and then, so that the completed liner could leave port, to deepen the channel by the removal of some 12 million square feet of earth and rock.

RIGHT: Four bronze screws, 16 feet in diameter, about to be mounted on shafts connected to support pinions that were an integral part of the hull.

ABOVE: Mounting the *Queen Mary*'s four-blade screws. Weighing 35 tons each, they were driven by four independent groups of action/reaction turbines with an overall 200,000 horsepower.

OPPOSITE: The rudder and screws of the *Aquitania*, launched in 1913 and not to be superseded in size and grandeur for more than twenty years.

Among the claims put forward to help a general public grasp the size of new ocean carriers, one of the most delightfully nutty is the boast of a German company, early in this century, that one of its new ships had a carrying capacity "in excess of the number of men engaged in the Seminole War of 1856–1858." Reaching for impressive figures and measurements, writers of brochures and reporters continued to provide hand-outs passed on to readers already benumbed with hyperbole. By the time the *Queen Mary* was launched, the contest between the ingenious and the awesome had come to a standstill. The *Mary*'s power, said one reporter, was calculated to be about equal to the muscle power of seven million galley slaves rowing in unison. The cables carrying electric energy through the ship, said another, were estimated to be 4,000 miles long, long enough to reach from New York to San Francisco and then some 800 miles out into the Pacific. The torch in the hand of the Statue of Liberty would barely top the roof of the *Queen Mary*'s bridge. The head of the Sphinx, in fact, would

not even come up to the main deck at the stern. The First Class dining room and foyer had enough cubic space to house the *Britannia*, Cunard's first transatlantic liner, and still have room to pack in beside her Columbus' *Nina*, *Pinta*, and *Santa Maria*. All by herself, the ship had a tonnage 22,000 more than that of the whole Spanish Armada. "I felt," said one news-paperman who saw her on the stocks, "like a fly crawling along the floor at the base of a hung carcass of Highland beef." For all the afflictions of nonsense she had to endure, the *Queen Mary* remains "the stateliest ship" in memory.

OVERLEAF: The four screws of the *France*, the last great transatlantic liner launched from a French shipyard. She was 1,035 feet in length, some 4 feet longer than the *Normandie*, with a tonnage of 66,348 and 160,000 horsepower. She worked the Le Havre–New York route at an average speed of 30 knots.

ABOVE: The *Queen Mary*, "a rampart of a ship,/Long as a street and lofty as a tower," in the words of Poet Laureate John Masefield, under construction at the John Brown Company shipyards at Clydebank, Scotland. With the *Normandie* already in service, thousands of laborers worked overtime to enable the British merchant marine to reassume pride of place.

The *Queen Mary*'s hull was separated into eighteen transverse compartments sealed by hydraulic doors; a double cellular bottom extended the length of the ship. The bow stem's upper portion was of molded steel plates, the lower of cast steel—a fact perhaps crucial to her survival. Travel-

ing in convoy on the North Atlantic, the *Mary* and the British cruiser *Curaçao* escorting her got their signals mixed. The breakdown in communications was calamitous: The great liner butted the little warship in the stern with a force that sent her spinning around at an angle of 90 degrees, then simply ran over her, slicing her in two like an apple. As 338 men suffocated in their bunks and hammocks, or drowned on the open water into which they were catapulted, the *Queen Mary*—under Admiralty orders never to put herself and her complement of men and matériel in jeopardy—plunged on.

ABOVE: The *France*, launched in 1962 (later the cruise ship *Norway*), during final stages of construction. Her smooth-sided hull is the result of the welding, rather than riveting, of steel plates. The bulbous forefoot adds buoyancy and helps keep the propellers wholly submerged in rough weather. The longest passenger ship ever built, she was never able to sail out of the shadow of the *Normandie*.

TOP: With their wives, Lord Abercombway of John Brown (Clydebank) Ltd. (*far left*) and Sir John Brockle-bank of the Cunard Steam-Ship Company Limited (*far right*) attend the ceremony in which the keel of the future *Queen Elizabeth 2* was laid. It was Lady Brocklebank (white hat and gloves) who had turned the Long Gallery of the *Queen Mary* into the Mid-ship Bar, thus replacing that stately adjunct to the main lounge with a suburban living room where fake windows were screened by jalousies and draped with flowered chintz. And it was she whose similar intentions for her husband's new vessel were thwarted only when a chorus of outrage from professional decorators, swelled by good-natured ragging on the part of newspaper column-ists, gave rise to the national scandal known as "Lady Brocklebank's Boo-Boo."

A few years later as, one by one, the *Queen Elizabeth 2*'s original London Gallery, Look-Out, or Observa-tion Lounge, and her Double Room's mezzanine were demolished to accommodate craps tables and slot machines, gimcrack boutiques and prefabricated penthouses with shag rugs, Murphy beds and gold-plated bathroom fixtures, many people longed for the return of her Ladyship's comparatively mild depredations.

OPPOSITE, BOTTOM: The hull and superstructure of the ship that will be christened *Queen Elizabeth 2* takes shape in the same Clydeside cradle from which the two previous *Queens* had emerged three decades earlier.

ABOVE: Not visible under the water, the shadow of the *Titanic* nevertheless continues to fall in a symbolic way upon it. The disaster that overtook her dissolved the myth of the unsinkable ship and contributed to a general lapse of confidence in the idea of scientific progress throughout the western world. In a minor but lasting way, her fate also impeded developments in the exterior design and possibly the safety of ships that would succeed her. Among the many scandals brought to light in the boardrooms where the causes of the *Titanic*'s demise were scrutinized, none more impressed the public than the revelation that, like almost every other passenger ship afloat, she did not carry lifeboats in sufficient numbers to accommodate her passengers, much less her crew. Certified to accommodate a total complement of 3,547, she had lifeboats for no more than 1,178. As a conse-

quence, agencies in charge of maritime safety made the number of lifeboats and their equipment and capacity a central issue; and the laws that ensued have been kept on the books long after lifeboats, in comparison with other means of survival at sea, have become obsolete. If lifeboats are essential to safety, it is argued, aircraft carriers and destroyers would have them.

Aware of this, James Gardner designed the *Queen Elizabeth 2* as the first liner to take advantage of inflatable rafts and other devices developed in the course of World War II, thus meaning to do away with the ugly port and starboard appendages of lifeboats-in-a-row that marred the clean sweep of line he was after. But the past reasserted itself; the British code of the sea in regard to lifeboats was unalterable, and Gardner was denied his opportunity to bring the design of merchant ships into line with advances that were already taken for granted on military vessels. The *Queen Elizabeth 2* is not the ship she might have been because the *Titanic*, idea and reality, was what she was.

31

Local events in the nineteenth century, launchings became days of national celebration in the twentieth. Cardinals and archbishops blessed hulls poised in launching slips; queens and the wives of presidents smashed beribboned magnums of champagne against them; church and state united to certify one more proof of tribal genius, while shipwrights waved caps and thousands cheered.

TOP: Dignitaries, descended from a barouche, arrive on March 21, 1905, for the launching of *La Provence* at Saint-Nazaire.

MIDDLE: Blessing *La Provence*. Built for service on the route between Le Havre and New York, *La Provence* had a gross tonnage of 13,752 and was nearly 630 feet long. Her 30,000 horsepower drove her at a speed of 25 knots. One of the fastest liners then at sea, she was the first French Line ship to be equipped with wireless telegraphy.

BOTTOM: Saint-Nazaire, twenty-seven years later. Mme. Albert Lebrun, wife of the president of France, christens the *Normandie* with champagne. Traditionally done by hand, and often with dismaying consequences—spattered costumes, missed connections, injuries to workmen and spectators below—christenings were later mechanized so that godmothers needed but to press buttons releasing bottles, swung on ribbons, into the ship's nose.

OPPOSITE: The launching of the *Europa*, one day before the launching of her sister ship and running mate, the *Bremen*, which she would outlive by nearly twenty years.

OVERLEAF: The launching in 1926 of the *Ile de France*, the first large liner built after World War I and the largest built by France up to that time. Here she slips into the Loire River on tons of smeared tallow, to be floated to the dock where she will be fitted out. During her thirty-two years of service, she would carry nearly a million passengers and, on nine occasions, go to the rescue of other ships in distress.

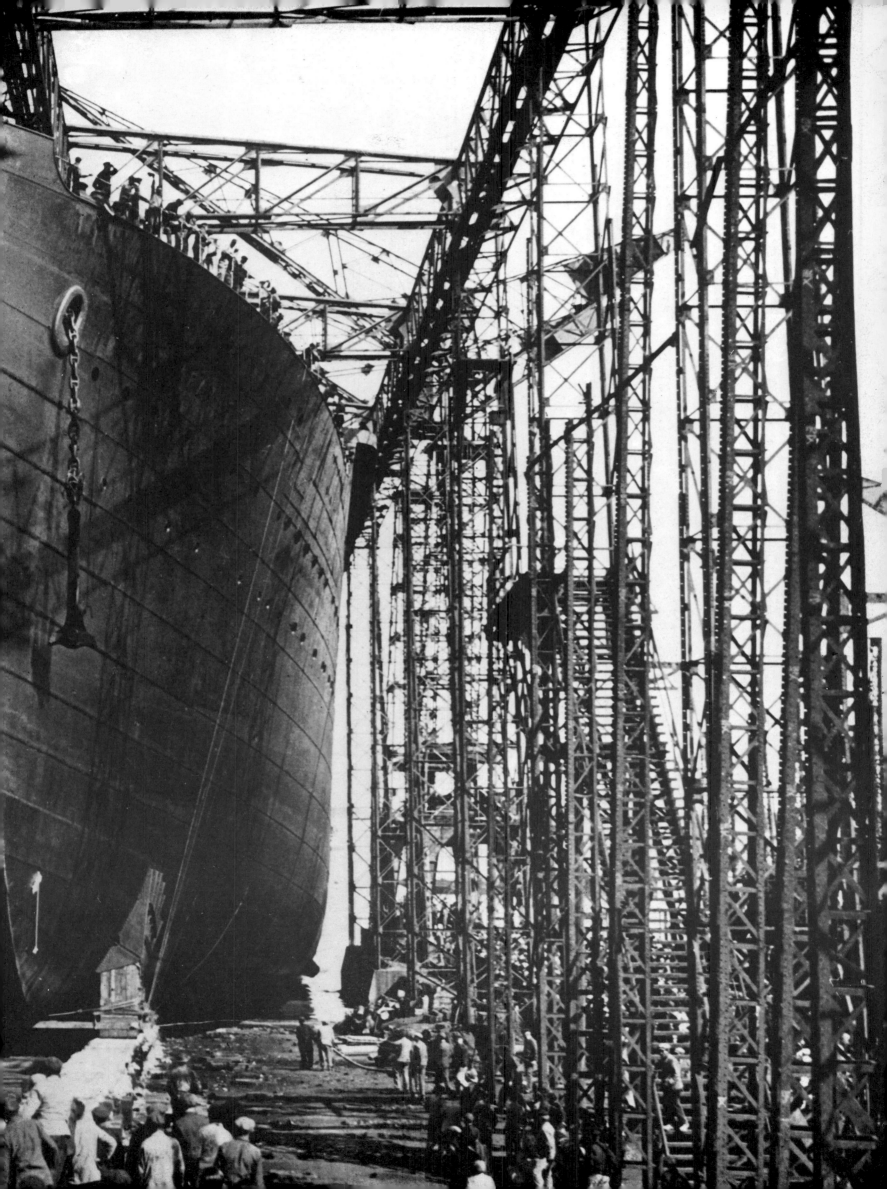

A good part of the drama of a launching lay in its brevity: One minute a structure as vast and formidable as a walled city towered above you, next minute it was entirely gone, leaving only enormous ribs of steel against the sky. This severance was always breathtaking—the monstrous thing that seemed to belong to the landscape as completely as anything else in sight was instantly parted from the land and given over to another element. On occasion, so were the souls who had come to witness. The *Normandie* pulled ninety workmen and spectators into the water after her; the *Queen Mary* inundated and left soaking the crowd lined up along the banks of the Clyde across from the stocks. No launching took place without recollection of disaster.

In 1909, when Italian shipbuilders launched the quadruple-screw *Principessa Jolanda*, destined for the Genoa–Buenos Aires run, the ship began to slide down stocks insufficiently tallowed. Friction produced flames and threw the delicate balance out of whack. Smoking backward into the water, the ship rolled over and sank.

In 1883, when the *Daphne* was ready for launching at Govan, not far from present-day Clydebank, nearly two hundred workmen, men and boys, went aboard in order to continue work on her interior as soon as she was waterborne. When she had made her slide into the water, a portside anchor that should have provided balance dragged some 60 yards. Thrown into a list that dislodged building materials stacked inside her, the ship was caught by river currents before she could right herself. Rolling onto her port side, she sank in deep water, drowning 124 of the men and boys trapped inside.

OPPOSITE: 1934. Named by Queen Mary, with King George V standing at her side, the *Queen Mary* has just been launched in a delicate operation involving the relation of gravity to a weight restrained until the last moment by electrically controlled supports, curbed by drag chains clamped to the hull and then, if necessary, released by three hydraulic rams on each side.

ABOVE: The *Queen Elizabeth*. Touching the water for the first time, she will be its supreme mistress and monarch for thirty years. Then—a slow boat to China at one-eighth of her power—she will limp into Hong Kong Harbor and soon thereafter, empty and in flames, succumb to the element she had ruled.

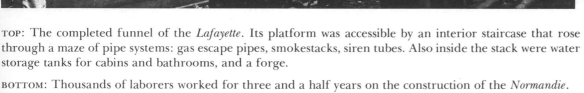

TOP: The completed funnel of the *Lafayette*. Its platform was accessible by an interior staircase that rose through a maze of pipe systems: gas escape pipes, smokestacks, siren tubes. Also inside the stack were water storage tanks for cabins and bathrooms, and a forge.

BOTTOM: Thousands of laborers worked for three and a half years on the construction of the *Normandie*.

OPPOSITE: The smokestacks of the *Normandie* nearing completion, surrounded by painters' scaffolding. By the end of the nineteenth century, the smokestack had become a symbol of prestige, some liners having as many as four, one of which might be a dummy. Such was the case with the *Normandie*'s third funnel, which served mainly as a kennel. Later ships, reluctant to dispense with funnels that had become supererogatory, kept them for aesthetic reasons, and found a function for them as solariums.

OPPOSITE: 1931. Jean Dunand and his son Bernard in a studio especially constructed for them to create the 30-foot silver-lacquered panels for the *Atlantique*. The studio later provided them with space to produce panels for the *Normandie*, one of which can be seen on page 210 (BOTTOM).

TOP: Workmen installing equipment in the "Mecanotherapy Salon" of the *Queen Mary*, where, on fixed contraptions, passengers could ride, bicycle, and row, or work out with punching bags and weights.

BOTTOM: Installation of the library aboard the *Queen Mary*. While cabinetmakers finish shelving, the librarian appears to be cataloguing books, even though his function, like that of every other ship's librarian, would be mainly to supply reference materials for quiz contests and sell postage stamps. Most seagoing libraries were either forbiddingly stodgy leather-bound collections of forgotten classics, or catch-as-catch-can selections from H. Rider Haggard, Zane Grey, and Warwick Deeping—until the advent of the *Queen Elizabeth 2*. On that ship's maiden voyage, the most spacious and beautiful library ever afloat offered passengers everything from Aristophanes to Zola in genuine classics, and shelf upon shelf—*Archaeology* to *Zionism*—of shiny-jacketed contemporary publications. Not long afterward, this superb room was dismantled and the space it occupied filled with rows of slot machines.

TOP: On April 25, 1914, the most awesome liner built up to that time, the *Vaterland* (later the *Leviathan*), flying the Hamburg American Line flag and guided by tugs, leaves the Blohm & Voss shipyards for her first trials on the open sea.

BOTTOM: The *Queen Mary*, fitted out and ready for her maiden voyage, leaves her building site to begin a delicate passage down the river Clyde into the Irish Sea.

OPPOSITE, TOP AND BOTTOM: The *Normandie* leaves the port of Saint-Nazaire for open water and her first speed trials.

OVERLEAF: On May 24, 1936, propelled by tugs, the *Queen Mary* moves downriver to Greenock. From there, once sea trials were over, she would head for Southampton, her home port. The tugboat operation, carried out under a heavy southeast wind in the narrow and twisting channel, did not proceed without mis- hap: The liner ran aground twice, once at the bow and once at the stern. Only after she had passed the last bend in the river, still guided by tugs, was she able to use her own propellers.

ABOVE: Arc lights show the *Ile de France* in floating dry dock. Once "the most direct route" between Greenwich Village and the Left Bank, this most eminent of ships ended her career far from home and in a state of degradation.

In 1959, when it became clear that she was no longer a paying proposition, she was sold for scrap to a firm in Osaka. Sailing out of Le Havre, her tricolor aloft, while a band played "The Marseillaise" and a few hundred people waved her goodbye, she started the long voyage to her graveyard. When she was out of sight, the French flag was lowered and the ensign of the Rising Sun run up. She became at once the *Furanzu Maru*, bound for the Orient.

When she got to Japan early in April, a sorry story came to light: A Hollywood movie producer had arranged with Okada Gumi, the owners of the Osaka scrapyard, to "hire" the *"Ile de France* at a cost of $4,000 per day, with the intention of blowing her up at sea in the interests of "dramatic

realism." Said this producer: "We do everything for real. When a boiler explodes, a boiler explodes. When a funnel collapses, bashing in the front deck, a funnel collapses and bashes in the front deck. Bulkheads really explode." The ship would not actually be sunk in midocean, he added, but in coastal shallows where she could be raised and given back to the scrapping firm.

The French Line, a bit late in the day, purported to be displeased, and so did the French government. Meanwhile, in a display of Nipponese finesse, the scrapyard firm made plans for a holy ceremonial of decommission. Invitations were sent out to the diplomatic corps in Tokyo, to leading figures in the shipping world, to naval attachés, and to individuals of high social standing. A Shinto altar was erected in the *Ile*'s First Class dining room, and, on the appointed day, food for the gods was laid out not far from a board of delicacies meant for the 1,000 people who turned up. When the assembled company had done its freeloading, a Shinto priest in

full ceremonial garb emerged to perform the rites of purification. Cleansed, spiritually immaculate, the beloved old *Ile de France* was then declared officially "dead."

Dead or alive, she was ignominiously dragged out to sea so that Dorothy Malone and Robert Stack might have the advantage of utter realism in a cinematic turkey entitled *The Last Voyage*. The ritual declaration of the *Ile*'s demise had in the meantime done nothing to placate the anguish of ship lovers. Expressions of outrage from all over the world prompted the French Line, backed up by the government, to demand that the name *Ile de France* not be visible in any movie-shot of the liner, under threat of banning the producer's pictures, now and forever, from French movie theaters. The name was removed under this pressure, but the cameras were not prevented from rolling. Brutally wrecked, burned, exploded, vandalized, and half-sunk, the old ship suffered ultimate depredation. Then, partially pumped out again, she was towed back to Osaka and, in the last reach of mercy, obliterated.

ABOVE: The *Queen Elizabeth 2* in drydock. Contrary to popular understanding, this ship is not named for the reigning monarch, Queen Elizabeth II, but for the great ship of the same name preceding her. Since the second *Elizabeth* was built in Scotland, where the legitimacy of Queen Elizabeth I is widely questioned, her owners considered it the better part of valor to designate the new liner by an arabic rather than a roman numeral and thus, they hoped, to make clear the fact that she was named for a retired ship and not a living person.

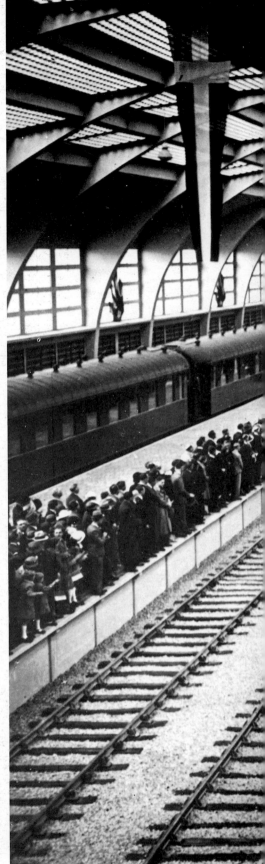

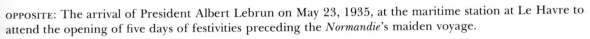

OPPOSITE: The arrival of President Albert Lebrun on May 23, 1935, at the maritime station at Le Havre to attend the opening of five days of festivities preceding the *Normandie*'s maiden voyage.

ABOVE, TOP: A gala dinner aboard *La Provence* of 1906, one of many liners whose careers were ended by torpedoes in World War I.

BOTTOM: Queen Elizabeth II visits the bridge of the *Queen Elizabeth 2*, accompanied by Commodore Bil Warwick, a Cunard official, and the Lord Mayor of Southampton. By this time the *Queen Mary* and *Queen Elizabeth* had been sold down the river in an auction-block transaction unsullied by sentiment on the part of their owners. Like most other steamship lines subsidized by governments, Cunard had over the years played the game two ways: When bankruptcy threatened, its ships were held to be wards of the state, mascots of the sentimental public, ambassadors of national honor deserving every kind of support—especially money; when a chance for unexpected profit loomed, its ships were suddenly private property to be dealt with privately and without regard for the noisy claims of the heirs of Nelson, the pathetic tears of flag-waving children, or the outrage of Empire widows.

Distress at the passing of the old standard-bearers was modified by hopes and expectations invested in the

new. She would be the miracle ship, the only one to outshine the heretofore peerless *Queens*, the one to recoup the glory of Britain on the seas. "The *Queens* are dead! Long live the *Queen*!" echoed through the millions of words written about the new ship even while she was still years away from the ceremonies that would launch her. By the time she was ready to slide down the ways, everyone from the royal family to the hucksters of Oxford Street had got into the act. The latter imprinted "*Q 4*," the working name of the still-unnamed ship, on razor blades, beer bottles, whiskey-flavored cake, gum, sweat shirts, dolls, and ball-point pens. Lord Snowdon turned up in the workrooms of designer Dennis Lennon to see what the First Class restaurant would look like. Interrupting her September holiday at Balmoral, Her Majesty and Prince Philip came down to Clydeside to

preside at the christening; Princess Margaret flew up from London to join them. On a festooned platform under the bulbous forefoot of the graceful monster, all three lifted their eyes as the great thrust of the bow was urged backward by gravity and the assistance of 9 tons of tallow, 70 tons of sperm oil, 14 hundredweight of black soap, and 7 gallons of spindle oil. "There are always too many people ready to knock and slam our country," Princess Margaret said when it was over, "and too many people wringing their hands over poor old Britain. But this new Cunarder will show that design in Britain is not only exciting and full of vigorous common sense but is always out in front, leading the field. A great ship like the *Queen Elizabeth 2* must inevitably be looked upon as a sort of flagship for the nation."

The second *France* leaves on her maiden voyage in 1912. She crossed to New York at a speed of 22.30 knots and made the return trip at 23.40, surpassed at the time only by the *Lusitania*'s and *Mauretania*'s 25 knots. With this ship the Compagnie Générale Transatlantique joined the ranks of important companies dispatching liners across the North Atlantic.

At about 24,000 tons, the *France* was considerably smaller than her German and British rivals but, like them, she sported, almost *de rigueur*, four big funnels. Sitting low in the water, she gave an impression of high style and efficient ease. "But she rolled like a sick headache," said one passenger; on her first voyage she broke thousands of dollars' worth of crockery. One of the *France*'s big and widely advertised features was the upgrading of the conventional *cabine de luxe* to an out-and-out *de grand luxe*, or "regal flat." These "princely suites of rooms" were large enough to accommodate six persons, thus allowing a family or a party of friends to cross the ocean "in complete isolation" from the *nouveaux riches* in conventional First Class and the *canaille* in other remote and obscure parts of the ship. Each suite had three canopied beds, and two others with brass

bedsteads. Its occupants had their own Empire-style dining room, a drawing room copied from a salon in a Touraine chateau, a bathroom, and "other domestic conveniences."

"Aboard the *France*," said one impressionable visitor, "one is even spared the tedious climb and descent of the staircase. The citizen of the floating town presses a button, a grille rolls back to reveal an elevator, and he is whisked to the desired floor." The same visitor was charmed by the saddlebag easy chairs in the smoking room and the refreshing waters of the swimming bath. "Even the luxury of a Turkish bath," he said, "is not denied to its votaries." On the dressing table in each of the expensive cabins, he noted, there was a "natty device" which "with the turn of a button" would allow a lady "to heat the intricate implements for completing the coiffure."

But one unreconstructed British connoisseur of seagoing amenities would not be taken in by such Gallic fripperies. French Line ships, he said, "are beautifully decorated, and fitted with every luxury; but they do not suit British taste, inasmuch as no notice is taken of the Sabbath day. The cuisine, wines, and attendance," he conceded, "are excellent."

THE GREAT CIRCLE
Leave-taking, Crossing, Landfall

First crossing or fiftieth, your fragile new identity would begin with a sight of funnels quietly smoking above Manhattan's West Side Highway. As your taxi crawled a crosstown street sloping toward the piers of the North River, you'd look for the particular one showing the colors of the house flag under which you'd chosen to sail—the red, white, and blue of the United States Lines; the raked little red, white, and blue hatband on the yellow funnels of the Norwegian American Line; the red, white, and green of the Italian; the French Line's somber red and black; the cap of red, white, and black painted on the yellow base of the Hamburg American Line's funnels; or, most distinctive of all, the renowned "Cunard red," a mixture of buttermilk and bright ocher topped by a broad black band and encircled with pencil-thin black lines. These colors had signified that line ever since Robert Napier, who "invented" them, supplied Samuel Cunard with engines for his early paddle-wheelers. They continued to do so until the designers of the *Queen Elizabeth 2* decided to paint their new ship's one smokestack black.

Excited and a bit ahead of yourself, you'd not likely be aware of your extraordinary door-to-dock convenience; you'd be sailing from a port that was not, as in most of Europe, a fairly remote gateway to a metropolis but part of a metropolis itself. Alongside the stanchions of the elevated highway, your taxi would pull up beside others parked four and five abreast disgorging passengers while heavyset men in long blue or beige bibs marked "Italia" or "Cunard" or "CGT" loaded suitcases and hatboxes onto hand-propelled trucks. These men were not, as the lettering on their bibs would have you believe, employees of foreign shipping lines. Their accents alone would mark them as longshoremen whose confiscation of your luggage would end only when, under a huge sign saying NO TIPPING, they waited while you fumbled for the dollars that would result in your bags being placed on a moving escalator. Up broad stairs, or into an elevator as big as a living room, you would gain the long broad pavilion of the pier open at both sides and hung with flags and banners like a medieval banquet hall. Your ship would be visible only as a wall of riveted plates and brass-ringed portholes as you proceeded to the cattle-pen enclosures and wooden structures marked First Class, Tourist Class, Third Class, or whatever designation had succeeded the old categories of Cabin, Second, and Tourist Third. Presenting your passage ticket and your passport to clerks from the shipping line's offices, you would be waved on to the gangplank—a canvas tunnel through which you would reach the ship's reception foyer and be greeted by white-jacketed stewards who'd escort you to your cabin.

Preoccupied, you would not have noticed that on open gangplanks leading to lower decks, cornucopian baskets of fruit from Charles & Co., roses in long boxes from Constance Spry, lavender tins of chocolates from Louis Sherry, and magnums of champagne from everywhere had come aboard when you did. (Nor would you have observed the quota of coffins which, just in case, went rumbling into the hold.)

In your cabin, you might find bon voyage gifts like these, along with boat letters, bar chits, telegrams, books of crossword puzzles, and *Guides Michelin*, as well as friends who had already consumed half the hors d'oeuvres you'd been thoughtful enough to order in advance and who were now waiting for you to break open the scotch you'd brought aboard. (The ban on the sale of spirits on ships in port, which, in the days of Prohibition, held good only until the famous twelve-mile limit, has been continued to this day as a regulation of U.S. Customs.)

Gusts of laughter from adjoining cabins would encourage you to do this at once and so become host to that ritual known as the sailing party. In later years, this would take place only during daylight hours. But before World War II, when midnight sailings were the rule, bon voyage gatherings were a familiar part of the social life of Manhattan, bringing glamour and merriment to departure scenes which, only a few decades earlier, had been marked by weeping and the remaking of wills, prayers and clinging last embraces. When midnight sailing parties became a nuisance for both crew and staff, the steamship companies did away with them. The trouble lay in getting celebrants ashore so that the ship might sail when she was supposed to. An hour before the gangplank was due to be pulled up, or mechanically pulled away, stentorian stewards would range throughout the ship calling the time-honored "All ashore who are going ashore!"—or some anacoluthic variation on those words—and underline the message by banging zealously on gongs. If you were sailing on an Italian ship, the message would be more urgent, less scrutable. There, as the novelist Shirley Hazzard has observed, the cry would be: "*La nave e in partenza!*" followed by its English translation, "The *sheep* is *living*!"

Taking fright at this, some visitors would flee down the gangplank. Others would ignore it as tumblers of Chivas Regal were refilled and champagne corks hit the overhead lights and there was nowhere to sit but on the bed or the bunk or the floor and everyone could still play house for another hour in a bright little room on the river at the end of West Forty-sixth Street. Cries of "The ship is about to sail . . . all visitors ashore!" would eventually disperse them, but not always. It became conventional to expect that some revelers, trapped on board and high as kites, would have to be returned in the sobering dark when the pilot boat parted from the ship at Ambrose Light.

By the mid-fifties, sailing parties had become comparatively subdued affairs ("security" reasons would altogether eliminate them in the early seventies), and embarking passengers were less apt to deal with guests than with arrangements to assure their comfort, or affirm their status, on the voyage. First among these was to consult with the Chief Steward and, heads together over a big seating chart, choose a well-situated and possibly congenial table in the dining room; then, in conference with the Chief Deck Steward, to secure a chair in a preferred location either on the covered promenade deck or on one of the open decks aft. Experienced travelers would see to these matters at once and so be free to explore the ship, case the glass-enclosed shelves of the library, and find a spot on the boat deck from which to view the casting off.

Until the middle of this century, sailing time was signaled not only by the clanging of metal but by the arrival on a pierside deck of a brass band with a repertoire that did not usually stray far from "Anchors Aweigh." Later, live musicians were replaced by recordings pumped through public-address systems; but the repertoire remained stubbornly as it was—"Sailing, Sailing, Over the Bounding Main," "Auld Lang Syne," the standards. As the band struck up, or the loudspeaker squawked, stewards bearing cornets of confetti and rolls of colored streamers would pass among passengers lined up three and four deep along the railings. Unrolled by a toss to the dock, these streamers in the hundreds would provide a last, paper-thin connection between people on shore and those about to depart. As the two audiences faced each other, shouting limp wisecracks and blowing kisses, a rumble from below would signal the removal of the gangplank and that ineluctable moment when, suddenly alive with a dynamo hum, the ship would be warped one inch from her moorings, then two. Looking straight down, a passenger could measure the already vast distance in the oily waters of the Hudson. Then, one by one, the streamers would break; one by one, the souls on board begin to turn in on themselves. As the ship backed out into the stream with accelerating speed, hundreds of people on the dock, trying to keep pace with her, would race to the open platform above the river. There they would wave handkerchiefs, lift infants onto shoulders, unfurl hitherto furled banners proclaiming love and bidding safe return. But ship-to-shore severance is absolute; by that time they would all have been forgotten.

Few passengers would ever stay on deck long enough to watch their ship's progress down the harbor and would thereby miss not only two of the fabled sights of the world but the incidental pleasures of its greatest port. Skyscrapers reaching up to form the jagged patterns made by glacier pinnacles on an *arête* are nowhere better seen than from a ship; and the Statue of Liberty, holding her torch to welcome the poor and homeless, also blesses the affluent and affirms their freedom to go. Miniature water traffic, crisscrossing the paths of a perpetual flotilla of cargo ships and the workaday lanes of ferry boats, continues all the way to the Verrazano-Narrows Bridge. And there, as you approach its humming cables, you become the subject of an optical illusion: dead certain that the masts and funnel of your ship are going to be sliced clean off at the top, you hold your breath until you've completely passed under. On the open boat deck and still able, as you will not be at sea, to view your ship in relation to something, you would be struck anew by the immensity of the "floating iron eggshell," as Sinclair Lewis's Dodsworth put it. Like him, you would look "along the sweep of gangways, past the huge lifeboats, the ventilators like giant saxophones, past the lofty funnels serenely dribbling black woolly smoke, to the forward mast."

Ambrose Lightship with its unending dirge (later replaced by Ambrose Tower with no loss of mournful music) was rendezvous—that point where, in swirls of brackish water, the tidal harbor meets the open sea. It was also the point of no return. Once the harbor pilot, swift as a spider, had climbed down his ladder of rope or made a leap from a lower deck onto his boat, your ship was on her own. As you'd watch the pilot boat cut its little arrow of a wake toward the skyscrapers of the Battery, you'd hear your liner's engines awakening like beasts in a cave. For the true seafarer, to feel her driving through land swells off Sandy Hook was an instant of exhilaration as his lungs filled with briny essences and a sudden lift of buoyancy caused him to stand, legs apart, asway against the horizon. But for another less romantically sea-struck, that moment would be a lurch into terror as his sense of balance disappeared and one inescapable and completely internal wave of yellow bile, streaked with puce, rose to eye level and overwhelmed him.

This victim, if he was lucky enough to be making his voyage no later than the middle of the twentieth century, would not have to suffer for long. Help from heaven would by that time have arrived in the hands of ministering angels—the physicians Leslie Gay and Paul Carliner of the allergy clinic of the Johns Hopkins University and Hospital. It was they who first spotted the efficacy of a synthetic antihistamine—$C_{17}H_{22}NO \cdot C_7H_6CIN_4O_2$, or dimenhydrinate—as a cure for seasickness, and they who took it to the Medical Corps of the United States Army for the massive testing which proved that fewer than 2 percent of passengers to whom Dramamine (the the market name of the formula) was administered were vulnerable to the affliction visited upon seagoing mankind throughout recorded history.

At lunch or dinner, first day out, "open sitting" would often be the case, providing a chance for you to catch at random the character and *ton* of at least a few of your shipmates. However, if things were not yet wholly in order—meaning that chefs and stewards had spent too many hours in the bar across the street from the head of the pier—and you were directed to the table assigned to you for the voyage, you would have come early to a moment of truth: the acquaintance of strangers with whom, for five days or nine, you would break bread, crack jokes, and show, or feign, that solicitude in little matters that comes easily to travelers who find themselves in the same boat. Lucky, you'd discover your tablemates to be outgoing, amenably reserved, or otherwise engaging. But if the necromantic intuition of the Chief Steward as he sized you up had somehow failed him and he had put you with individuals whose opinions and behavior you found disagreeable, perhaps appalling, you would have to take steps to be removed from their company, and to take these at once. The Chief Steward would, of course, not believe the excuses you would have made up to disguise your distaste, and would not be interested in them. He'd find you another table, the cost of which would be the contempt of those still seated at the table you had spurned, and the frozen stares with which they'd greet you on deck for the rest of the trip.

According to the printed program of the day's activities placed in your cabin, you could, after dinner, go to a movie, dance in the lounge that served at night as a ballroom, perhaps catch the Swiss juggler, the Neapolitan tenor, or the stand-up comedian from the borscht circuit offered as entertainment. But merriment on the first night out would be difficult to come by. A kind of spiritual pall would dominate your ship simply because, like you, your fellow passengers would have found themselves in a hiatus between the security of the life they'd only that morning left and the unfamiliarity of the life on which they had embarked. Instead of fox-trotting across a dance floor, they'd be rereading boat letters and telegrams, tallying like blessings the fruit and flowers that had endowed their staterooms with reminders of home, and fingering gifts from acquaintances whom, it now seemed, they should have taken more seriously.

Next morning, all this would change because conditions would have changed. Prevented from doing what you usually did, you would be dependent on strangers for the simplest kinds of guidance and look toward those in charge of the ship to give coherence to your new existence. With nothing to see but the sea, you'd realize that you were really on a floating island, that maybe you had something in common with Robinson Crusoe: If you were going to make insular survival possible, you'd have to accomplish this with available resources. But there the connection with Crusoe would end: Your steward, dancing in with a many-splendored breakfast on a tray, would give you a smile, a Passenger List, and an engraved invitation to the Captain's Reception that very evening.

The Passenger List—a talisman of identity, a roster of possibilities. Whether your intentions were erotic, directed toward social advantage, or merely the fulfillment of curiosity, this was your little tasseled bible and checklist. On British ships, passenger listings were apt to read like reductions *ad absurdum* of Burke and DeBrett and the *Almanach de Gotha*. Titles you might recognize, initials designating the recipients of obscure degrees and honors, each had their place in a caste system openly advertised. On other ships, when the Passenger List designated no more than name and gender, you'd be led to search for past acquaintances, or celebrities, or persons still unknown whose listings indicated they were unattached. In any case, the Passenger List was the one sure document of your presence at sea. Its abolishment by the overseers of the Cunard Line was just one of the unhappy innovations that came to ocean travel with the *Queen Elizabeth 2*.

"Getting there is half the fun" was that company's slogan until it was foolish enough to replace it with "Ships have been boring long enough"—thereby putting doubts in the minds of potential passengers to whom such an idea had never remotely occurred. Yet a voyage that might be "half the fun" was an attractive promise and one that it had been possible to keep from those years, roughly 1905 to 1914, when marine designers transformed liners from earnest ocean carriers without frills into pleasure palaces afloat. The idea was to offer voyagers a transatlantic passage during which, taking the slightest care to avoid contact with the elements, they might never be reminded they were at sea. Scrupulously advanced as the years went on, the idea was ultimately realized in full when, pressed by his clients, the great designer James Gardner removed from his plans for the *Queen Elizabeth 2* the open promenade that had been the joy of sea lovers for a hundred years. In its stead was constructed "a cradle to catch the sun," an afterdeck area which, on crossings between New York and Southampton, the winds of the North Atlantic would render almost permanently empty.

But if "half the fun" had little to do with the pleasure of those who loved the sights and sounds of the ocean as their ship made its way up and down the Great Circle, it had a lot to do with passengers to whom a transatlantic crossing was an anesthetizing experience made tolerable only by extraordinary creature comforts and entertainment laid on. Grandiose and socially topheavy, persistent as dinosaurs in their embrace of oblivion, the great ships came to their apogee by 1914, entered a postwar sunset phase in the 1920s, and, in spite of the undreamed-of size of the two Cunard *Queens* and the French Line's *Normandie*, never quite recovered the status and panache that once made them the visible wonders of the western world. By the early twenties, their characters had come to be defined less by designers than by the needs of a society which, in comparison with old rigidities of class and kind, was increasingly democratized, homogenized, and subject to the fantasies of the adman.

But such concerns would be of no account to a passenger who, one day out, would be passing through the first of three commonplace phases of response to his shipmates: revulsion, toleration, devotion. Revulsion would be immediate and unqualified: One look around the crowded deck and he might ask himself by what twist of fate he had been led to lay out good money to spend the next five days with this frumpy horde of nonentities. Toleration would make a tentative appearance a day or so later. Well fed, a bit bored, ready to take another look around, the passenger might begin to exchange weak smiles and muffled greetings with the people at the next table or in the adjoining deck chairs. Not a bad crowd, all considered, he would say to himself; or to his wife, "Why don't we ask those nice people from North Chagrin for a drink before dinner?" Devotion would follow. Three days out on a shining sea, rested, bemused, and indolent, our typical passenger would hardly be aware that total dismay had been replaced by wonder. By what blessed providence had so many lovely people found themselves on the very same ship?

Yet acquaintances struck up on crossings were inevitably fleeting. No matter how carefully shipmates might plan for eventual reunion on land, the occasion would be lost to contingency or indifference. Like an event in chemistry, shipboard friendships or romances could take place only when a particular set of conditions prevailed. To those who swore devotion to their new friends in the midships bar or the smoking room, nothing would be more unsettling than to have them turn up—obstreperous strangers at the front door—three months later.

Romance. Somewhere in the 1920s, there emerged a myth of shipboard dalliance in which the lifeboat came to be the place of tryst. Hollywood and the popular press promoted the notion, and the landlocked public bought it. To new seafarers with an eye to erotic privacy beyond the purview of cabinmates or ubiquitous stewards, the myth must have been the cause of many a wincing disappointment. There undoubtedly were impromptu embraces in the tarpaulined confines of lifeboats, but as passion pits they were not to be recommended. Except for those to whom oil, grease, hawsers, and mildew were aphrodisiac, the lifeboat was the last resort.

Breakfast over, the great labyrinthine vessel was yours to explore, its activities yours to join or decline. Shipmates bent on keeping fit would have already done a brisk mile around an open deck or, led by the physical director (who was also the masseur), kicked and twisted themselves into shape through a series of barked-out exercises. Others, in a group, would be taking lessons from one of the team of dance instructors who doubled as entertainers. Still others would have found the library and a waterside corner in the lounge, or been tucked into deck chairs. Among the latter would be inveterate travelers by sea who found in shipboard life the most satisfying formula for contented existence: endless activity, which they could scrupulously ignore. Neither athletes nor devotees of Jane Austen, they would have settled for that exposure to the elements known as the "sea cure," and for the amusement of the passing scene. Bundled in blankets from which they could study the ship's wake and the deportment of fellow passengers, they would have joined that deck-chair camaraderie in which nothing more than simple good manners opened the way to social opportunities and romantic attachments and, in some instance, financial killings. Ernest Hemingway met Marlene Dietrich on the *Ile de France*. Thomas Wolfe first encountered Aline Bernstein, the love of his life, on the *Olympic*. And it was the art dealer Lord Duveen of Millbank who made a science of what, in the matter of shipboard mateyness, had long been purely fortuitous.

Early on in his forty years of transatlantic crossings, Duveen developed an ingenious technique. Arriving on board, he would scan the passenger list for names identified with wealth in a sufficient amount to be worth his pursuit, and pick out the one that seemed most likely. On deck before anyone else, the hundred-dollar bill in his hand conspicuously visible, he would ask a deck steward to see that his chair was placed directly next to that of his chosen prey. Wrapped in steamer rugs, sharing morning bouillon and afternoon tea, Duveen and his neighbor would soon be familiars on their way to becoming parties to business deals. One of the clients Duveen met in this fashion, the carpet tycoon Alexander Smith Cochran, turned out to be good for $5 million worth of European art. Aboard the *Aquitania*, Duveen's elegant opportunism again paid off. "Finding" himself in accommodations adjoining the Gainsborough Suite occupied by the railroad magnate H. E. Huntington, he promptly maneuvered discussion to the copy of *The Blue Boy* hung in the suite's dining room. Within months, kindly guided and counseled by Duveen, Huntington was the owner of the original *Blue Boy*, at a profit to his lordship of $620,000.

Associations like Lord Duveen's belonged to an era when society was a comparatively small and clearly defined entity, when the rich most openly flaunted their privilege and most confidently moved among their kind. On the *Titanic*, for instance, every fourth or fifth family among First Class passengers brought with it a maid, a valet, and a nurse or a governess. At a time when the annual income of an average American family was well below $1,000, numbers of that ship's unlucky passengers paid well over $4,000 for passage tickets; partly because, for that social season, the maiden voyage of the *Titanic* was *the* thing to do. In their bouffant hairdos and corsets, high collars and high-buttoned shoes, ancestors of the jet set had come flocking from all over the Continent to embark at Cherbourg or Southampton. "No one consulted the Passenger List," said one déclassé observer. "They met on deck as one big party."

When society came to absorb café society, or vice versa, an old hegemony was broken. But in the consequent easier mix of things, one of the pleasures of transatlantic travel continued to be its inevitable element of serendipity. When you bought a ticket for Naples on the new *Leonardo da Vinci*, who'd have thought it would include evenings on the dance floor with honeymooners Richard Burton and Elizabeth Taylor? That invitation to cocktails in the Captain's quarters on the *Queen Mary*—who could have guessed it would find you discussing with Leopold Stokowski the difference between Dover sole and Cherbourg sole? On the *Queen Elizabeth 2*'s first eastward crossing, was it cupidity or charity that led your steward to place your deck chair next to Lord Mountbatten's? What about that table for one you settled for on the *Michelangelo*'s last westward voyage and then relinquished, simply because the Duchess of Windsor, observing your solitary splendor, asked you to join hers? When you booked an August crossing on the *United States*, how could you have known in advance that your entertainment of an evening would be provided by your shipmate Bob Hope? That September voyage on the *Ile de France*, what confluence of chance or taste allowed you to turn the pages of the Passenger List and, even before you'd left Le Havre, count among its names thirty-seven people whom you already knew, and those of Virgil Thomson and Samuel Goldwyn whom you were about to meet?

Unaware, first day out, of just what your voyage might hold in store, you would automatically submit to its routine. Bouillon and biscuits at eleven—once brought to deck chairs by stewards but in recent years laid out on come-and-get-it trolleys—remained an absolute of the sea lanes. Then, at noon sharp, a blast of the ship's whistle, jolting you upright, would send you to one of the bars, where, as far as you could tell, some of those on bar stools had already been there for days, including women of congenial disposition whose opening remarks would be spoken before you could decide on yours. (Alcoholics kept a secret: Only they knew that one of the few places where a hard-drinking woman could drink as much as she pleased without censure, if not without eventual detection, was a ship's bar.) In the buzz of newly made acquaintance, stewards would be selling tickets on the day's run, another ritual of the voyage, which, in some instances, might reward successful bettors with cash in an amount to cover all the expenses of the crossing, including the passage ticket. Then the luncheon gong would send you to a table where the austere strangers you first laid eyes on yesterday would exchange with you greetings suggesting you'd known one another since childhood and would forever stay fast friends.

By midafternoon, the social hostess would have come into her own; the card room filled with bridge players, the sports deck echoing with the click of the discs used in shuffleboard, the promenade deck aft with the pock-a-pock of Ping-Pong balls. While the movie in the theater would unreel before hundreds of empty seats, the chairs in the beauty parlor would swivel for one customer after another.

Culminating in the Captain's Dinner, the first day's program would include not only a generous hour or so for tea in the lounge but sessions of bingo or horse racing, the latter managed by stewards who, at the throw of dice, moved little cutouts of thoroughbreds affixed to standards toward a finish line; sometimes, in later years, your bet would be decided by motion pictures of actual races photographed at American tracks. These gatherings, allowing everyone aboard to see almost everyone else, were designed less for serious gambling than for conviviality. In the last years of the great *Queens* of the Cunard Line, such introductory entertainments were put aside because there were just not enough people traveling in First Class to provide a participatory quorum. Tea time, still honored in regal style, was apt to be an occasion more indicative of the moribund state of things than of the tradition it meant to uphold. It was then possible for you to turn up for tea in the dim depths of the grand saloon and sit, magnificently alone, while a dozen white-jacketed stewards stood about like sentries, alert to your command. As you chose cucumber sandwiches, cakes, and scones from portable caddies, as all the pyramidal napkins on all the tables in the gloaming multiplied your sense of isolation, a shadowy figure at the far end of the room would seat himself at the Wurlitzer. Then, as the great ship plunged and rolled a thousand miles from land, the intruder would shiver the air with selections from *Rose Marie* and *The Desert Song*. Not even the dining room in *Citizen Kane* was emptier.

The official start of the voyage was the Captain's Dinner, preceded by a cocktail party in the main lounge. In your formal clothes, you'd come to a reception line where the social hostess would present you to the ship's officers one by one until you came to the Captain himself. Photographers would immortalize the moment of your handshake (for which, next day, you might secretly pay a large sum for half a dozen cardboard-framed prints). And only a moment it would be, since the Captain was invariably a man trained in the art of forestalling conversation and in giving your hand just that exquisitely subtle twist of welcome-and-dismissal that would not tempt you to linger. In any case, no matter who you were or where you came from, you would have been afforded a moment of equality with your shipmates and a moment of recognition, however glazed, by the man whose services you had paid for and into whose hands you had entrusted your life.

The Captain's duty to cater to the self-regard of his clientele made it essential that he be a social arbiter. Once his ship's safety was assured, he was expected to act as host and do all in his power to induce his guests to travel again in the same ship or in another of the line. It was his role, said one Captain, "to adjust disputes, pacify angry women, comfort frightened ones, and judge correctly just when to send one whose conduct is questionable to her room for the rest of the passage. He must know when to forbid the bartender to serve more liquor to a passenger who is drinking too much and just when to post the notice in the smoking room that gamblers are aboard. Passengers must not be antagonized unless they antagonize others more valuable to the company than themselves, for the company exists to carry the public over the ferry, not to better their morals. A master, under English maritime law, is a magistrate at sea. He may, if he wishes, perform marriages on board, and such ceremonies are as binding as though performed on shore. He may put the line's president and board of directors in irons if they interfere with the navigation of the ship, and though it is probable that he will soon be out of a berth if he pursues such courses, he will suffer no legal punishment."

With his Purser, the Captain had to pore over *Who's Who* and the tip-off lists from the home office before he could select that "frieze of simulated order" that would make up the Captain's Table, or prepare the roster of others who, having paid for the most expensive staterooms available, naturally expected that, sometime during the voyage, the Captain would request the pleasure of their company. In spite of meticulous preparation, the Captain's Table on any crossing tended, by and large, to reflect his own personal tastes, perhaps his own ambitions. Over aristocrats of birth and title, or members of the community of arts, letters, and the professions, most captains preferred the company of the conspicuously rich—men whose identities were inseparable from their corporations, free-floating women whose distinction was estimated in the number of trunks that had accompanied them to the dock. One commander put the matter succinctly: "Although the Company never exert any pressure as to who is to sit where, there is naturally a tendency to consider its commercial interests where influential passengers are concerned."

The many-shelved library of memoirs by retired captains of the great liners confirms a suspicion that nearly all of them were yokels in braid: men with horizons limited to what their binoculars might explore and to what, otherwise, the company man's vision could discreetly encompass. Contrary to all they had, perforce, to witness in the way of jostling for privilege, arrogant shows of what money can buy, drunken bad manners, the gaping yawns of businessmen trussed up in their soup-and-fish, women groaning at the weight of diamond earrings and the pinch of jeweled slippers, their social commentaries were often indistinguishable from the blurbs of travel folders. "Hundreds of multicolored fairy lamps," said one of them, "shed their soft radiance on the forms of beautiful women gloriously gowned and handsome men in immaculate evening dress who dance the hours away to the music provided by jolly orchestras."

Accomplished seamen up from the ranks, captains had to train themselves to act with a social grace for which few of them had the background, disposition, or aptitude. Yet their pragmatic view of the ways of the world sometimes gave them sharp insight into the social stratum they entered voyage to voyage. "Rich men," said one skipper, "spend their lives ashore at work and once it is put aside they become as bewildered as dogs who have temporarily mislaid their masters." But, more often than not, the autocrats of the Great Circle were as giddy as schoolboys in the presence of multimillionaires, prizefighters, and ladies whose widely publicized divorces had left them with as many names as their clinking bracelets had charms.

Psychologically speaking, the great advantage of shipboard life was the feeling, three days out, that you had never lived anywhere else but in a crisp, well-ordered little cabin kept neat by invisible hands and a conviction that you had never had to deal with anything more pressing than options for amusement. The rhythm of your days would have become as constant and unvarying as the ship's. With your worries limited to what to wear, how to take in the movie matinee and still have time for a rubber of bridge before cocktails in the Captain's quarters or the Purser's, you would have little thought for the hazards of the ocean and no expectation of being confronted by them.

You would have studied the printed notice on your stateroom door instructing you to be alert to signals meaning fire on board, or abandon ship; and you would have noted its photograph of a man in a life preserver, upon whose face doom was already written large. Putting on your life jacket, you may even have joined the lifeboat drill a few hours out, got to your muster station, seen your particular lifeboat, and been told what to do should you find yourself adrift in icewater. Puffed up in your orange jacket and as Humpty-Dumpty as anyone else, you may have made fun of a legal requirement that otherwise might have been too morbid a reminder of disasters and close calls.

While nautical technology advanced step by step into a computerized dispensation, the North Atlantic had meanwhile retained its calamitous unpredictability. One summer evening in 1957, in a mere acre or so of fog, the *Stockholm*'s swordfish prow knifed into the side of the *Andrea Doria* and sent her rolling to the bottom. A year earlier, on a voyage from Genoa to New

York, the *Michelangelo* encountered one of the almost inexplicable mountainous crests of water which, every ten years or so in the history of steamships, have broken over the masts and funnels of even the greatest of liners. Often, in calm seas, they have come out of nowhere—single waves of such power as to throw a ship into a list almost beyond righting. Sometimes they have come, like a *coup de grace*, as a ship was battling the worst gale force of the Atlantic. In the *Michelangelo*'s case, it was the latter. Moving through wild seas, the 900-foot length of her seemed to those aboard to be actually whipping back and forth, as though she might at any moment snap in two. As terrified passengers were flung from their beds and bunks, or sent crawling along galleyways, forced to "cling together like a cluster of grapes," a few others still tried to carry on the normal life of a ship at sea. Among these was the German novelist Günter Grass. He was chatting with some shipboard acquaintances in a lounge when one of them, a man from Chicago, said he wanted to watch the storm from the big windows of his upper-deck stateroom. Grass and the others, invited to join him, felt they should stay where they were. Their friend went to his cabin and was killed, perhaps instantly, when the towering wave battered down the forward wall and with one overwhelming blow wrecked the bridge, the officers' quarters, and twenty First Class staterooms. A second passenger and a member of the crew also perished under its impact; a woman wedged into the debris of her wrecked cabin was saved by crewmen who cut a hole in the door with axes only after water had poured into the room up to her waist. The *Michelangelo* came into New York like a funeral barge. Her flag flew at half mast, and over the ruined front of her was stretched, like a bandage, an enormous tarpaulin.

For those passengers who'd gained sea legs, a tempest midocean could be a welcome break in the monotonous constancy of a ship's passage, a chance to stand foursquare and, in perfect confidence, brave the elements. For others it would mean precipitate retreat, to a familiar corner of the bar or to bed. Only in rare cases would a storm cancel the published program of the day. Musicians might have to play into the empty space of vast lounges filled with little but the creakings of paneled walls; open decks might be rolling awash and dining rooms seem but ghostly exhibitions of napery and tableware; but the schedule of events would be kept. Most people could take the roll of a great ship (the *Kaiser Wilhelm der Grosse* was nicknamed "the Rolling Billy," and, until she got stabilizers, the *Queen Mary* was famous for her whalelike wallowings from side to side), but few could tolerate the pitch. When these were combined and the ship, propellers spinning in air, seemed suddenly to be standing on her head, even passengers whose inner ears were atrophied by some form of dimenhydrinate were likely to feel themselves dizzily retreating into stupor.

From a financial point of view, most of the great ships still in the water after World War II did well enough, year after year, to set up expectations that they might continue to be major transatlantic carriers for decades to come. But in the late 1950s, pure jets—as distinguished from jet-assisted planes like the Britannia—began to streak through the troposphere from New York to London and Paris in six and a half hours. The message they wrote in vapor trails was clear: The age of the passenger liner on the North Atlantic had come to a close. Sea travel did not so much decline or diminish as plummet, almost out of sight. The uneasy balance between sea and air, maintained for a few transitional years, went wildly out of kilter. Hawks in for the kill, the jets took over—to such an extent that, by the late 1960s, for every twenty-four passengers who went to Europe, only one of them went by sea. This one recidivist and his antiquarian shipmates were not exactly a pitiful minority. Frightened by the cattle-count logistics of airlines and airports as much as by flying itself, they were not afraid to spend unconscionable sums to travel quite as they still wanted to. The steamship era's holdovers and latecomers, they were prepared for a last stand, if only they could find where to make it.

On the *Queen Elizabeth*, for instance, the Captain's Reception had become both an occasion for uneasy gaiety and an index to despair. The ladies and gentlemen of the First Class would, by custom, dress up for the second-night-out assembly that signified the social beginning of the voyage. As they lifted their third curl of smoked salmon and their fourth dry martini from the salvers held out to them, Commodore Geoffrey Thrippleton Marr himself would mount a dais and tap his glass for attention. In a set speech that regular voyagers were used to, he would congratulate them, first for having chosen the sea over the sky, then for the charming carelessness about money that had brought them entrée into the great lounge where they were gathered that evening, and finally for the good taste that had led them to prefer Cunard. There would always be a few people like them, he suggested, lovers of life on the ocean wave and devotees of Beluga caviar, who would resist being hurried into metal cylinders and sent soaring across the Atlantic night just for the sake of "saving" a few days. At these doughty words the assembled company would clap hands and cheer. As cries of "Bravo!" and "Hear! Hear!" rose among the great pillars, one could hear the echoes of gladiators in the Colosseum: *Morituri*, said the blue-haired ladies and balding gentlemen, *te salutamus*. Then, as stewards began to brush away crumbs and to bring in balloons and streamers for the Get-Together Dance later on, they would all disperse. Weaving slightly under the influence of Beefeater gin, some would go down to the ice sculptures and cornucopian fruit baskets at the entrance to the restaurant, others up to the shaded lamps and flambéed chafing dishes of the Verandah Grill. A few years later, packed even more closely together than their forebears had been packed into steerage, most of them would go to Europe in Boeing 747s. Commodore Marr, meanwhile, part curator, part caretaker, would be spending the long Florida days in the limbo of Port Everglades watching over the echoing emptiness of the biggest ship in the world as it awaited its final disposition.

ARRIVAL

> *Here is a coast; here is a harbor;*
> *here, after a meager diet of horizon, is some scenery . . .*

wrote Elizabeth Bishop, and went on to document what any man or woman arriving at an unfamiliar port might feel:

> *Finish your breakfast. The tender is coming,*
> *a strange and ancient craft, flying a strange and brilliant rag.*
> *So that's the flag. I never saw it before.*
>
> *I somehow never thought of there being a flag,*
> *but of course there was, all along. And coins, I presume,*
> *and paper money; they remain to be seen.*

Landfall could be sensed off the coast of Ireland in a curious breath of air, a waft of peat smells and smoke, long hours before land was in sight. Off France or England, more often than not, it would be evident in a kind of rain heavy with the effluvia of tidal zones. Off Portugal and Spain, dry winds would carry the odors of bark and burned earth to tell you that the great blue shoulders of the Pillars of Hercules were about to come into view. That close, little fishing boats singly or in pairs, or tied to one another like circus elephants, trunk to tail, would have confirmed the imminence of your arrival and set up emotions for which you were unprepared.

For a week or more you had inhabited an artificial but entirely diverting and secure little world of which you were now a full-fledged citizen. All at once, it was going to turn you out, allowing you not even time to sort out your feelings. As, in unfamiliar street clothes, you'd come to your last meal, there to exchange addresses with friends you'd never see again, your luggage would already be stacked outside your cabin, your attention neither wholly here nor there. Unable to project yourself into tomorrow, or find the means to cling to today, you would be in the state described by Cecil Day Lewis:

> *When the dazed heart*
> *Beats for it knows not what, whether you part*
> *From home or prison, acquaintance or lover—*
> *Something wrong with the time-table, something unreal*
> *In the scrambled meal*
> *And the bag packed by the door, as though the heart*
> *Had gone ahead, or is staying here forever.*

Usually scheduled for a morning hour, disembarkation was invariably a tedious process as you showed up in long queues in the lounge to have your passport checked by officials who'd brought their briefcases aboard, then found yourself dogged by a forgotten steward—perhaps "the shoes," as the British called the bootblack, whose nocturnal presence had never disturbed you, *or* your shoes—alert for a tip; and otherwise being harassed by voices over loudspeakers demanding that you hearken to announcements having nothing to do with you.

Leaving your ship by tender at Cobh or Plymouth or Cannes, you would at last be able to grasp her immensity. Shadowed by the great wall of riveted plates against which the tender would rub like a piece of flotsam, you might for the first time realize that, all along, you had been a passenger on a ship at sea and not merely an overactive guest at a seaborne summer hotel. If you were warped by tugboats into one of the great maritime pavilions at Southampton, Le Havre, or Naples, there would be no time to look back; boat trains would be waiting to bear you into the interior.

In either case, free of that jet-lag-induced split that can keep body and soul apart for days, you would have arrived, hale and rested, all in one piece.

LEAVE-TAKING

The Port of Liverpool: four large White Star and Cunard liners with the tall smokestacks that were typical just before and just after World War I. Until 1920, Liverpool was England's largest port, but its docks were not deep enough to accommodate the new seagoing giants. Southampton, with more suitable facilities and easier access to London, became the home port for nearly all big British ships except those sailing to Canada.

TOP: The Port of Marseilles in 1905, departure point for ships crossing the South Atlantic to Mexico, Brazil, and Argentina.

BOTTOM: The Port of Hamburg, formerly known as Kaiser Wilhelmshafen, was home for ships of the Hamburg American Line.

TOP: The marine terminal at Le Havre, opened in 1935, had nearly a mile of deepwater docking facilities.

BOTTOM: In the Port of New York are, left to right, the *Queen Mary*, the *Parthia*, the *Liberté*, and the *Ile de France* (after having had her three original funnels reduced to two). "Steamship Row," where as many as ten liners were sometimes visible from mid-Manhattan windows, would soon not only be bereft of transatlantic carriers but lose its familiar cruise ships to Port Everglades, Miami, and San Juan.

TOP: The afterdeck of the *Normandie*; to the left, the *Paris*; to the right, the *Colombie*, which ran regularly to the islands of the French West Indies.

BOTTOM: At the London docks, loading the forward hold of the *Delta*, a cargo-cum-passenger ship of the P&O Line.

TOP AND BOTTOM: Automobiles of diverse function and vintage
suspended midair before being lowered into the hold.

TOP AND BOTTOM: Automobiles entering the garage of the *Normandie* by manpower.

OPPOSITE, TOP: The mail-carrying hydroplane ready to be loaded on board.

OPPOSITE, BOTTOM: Mailbags.

When the *Ile de France* made her bow in 1927 she was, to one observer, the picture of "imposing dignity and curiously old-fashioned grace." But she was not stodgy. A year later, one indisputably new thing about her was the clutter of a plane-launching catapult installed on her afterdeck. This contraption was designed as a means of shortening the delivery of trans-oceanic mail by a full twenty-four hours. It worked so well that the dramatic torpedolike launching of a plane—one day out from New York or Le Havre—was part of the entertainment of a crossing for more than two years. The maiden flight of this

(*continued on following page*)

73

(*continued from preceding page*)

service took place on August 12, 1928. When the liner was still 400 miles northeast of Sandy Hook, nearly all of her passengers gathered on the boat deck to witness the birth of a new era. In leather and goggles, Lieutenant Louis-Marie Demougeot and his radioman climbed into a Lioré & Oliver biplane and sat there waiting while everyone held his breath. Then with an ear-shattering detonation the thrust of the catapult sent them high out over the foaming wake of the *Ile*. As their 480-horsepower Gnome and Rhone Jupiter engine took hold, they dipped back, circled the ship to waving handkerchiefs and applause from all classes, and disappeared toward the American shore. Three hours and seven minutes later they splashed down near Quarantine in New York Harbor, delivered up their mailbags, and went into Manhattan to await the arrival of their shipmates on the following day.

Not long afterward the *Bremen* was fitted with a similar plane-launching device. The next logical thing seemed to be landing space on liners that would save a day at each end of the voyage for passengers as well as for mail. "The fast mail liner of the future," went one prediction, "may well be built with an immense flight deck, like that of an aircraft carrier, on which a swarm of her own planes will alight when the ship is clear of the Channel, to rise again when she is nearing New York, and carry important travelers to their destination."

Loading goods and supplies before embarkation, including 90 tons of ice. Kitchen personnel on the *Liberté* numbered 187 cooks and assistants, along with nine butchers, ten bakers, six wine stewards, fifteen pastry cooks and confectioners.

Cold-storage items on the *Normandie* (OPPOSITE PAGE AND ABOVE, TOP) and on the *Queen Mary* (BOTTOM). Publicity releases in both France and England often suggested that these nations existed mainly to provision their great ships. Nevertheless, hyperbole and fact were, in actuality, closely related. On her maiden voyage in May 1935, the *Normandie*'s storerooms and refrigerator chambers contained 60,000 eggs, 4,000 chickens, 1,000 squabs, 8,000 ducks, 4,000 turkeys, 1,200 pigeons, 300 rabbits, over 20,000 pounds of beef, 4,400 pounds each of veal, mutton, and lamb, 1,200 loins of pork, 4,400 pounds of ham, and nearly 9,000 pounds of specialty meats. Her wine cellars stocked 24,000 bottles of wine, 7,000 of *grand cru* and champagne, 2,600 of various liqueurs, beer, and mineral water.

The port of embarkation for many emigrants was Hamburg. Responding to pitchmen dispatched by the steamship companies to remote areas of Russia, Poland, and the countries of Mittel-Europa, they arrived by the hundreds of thousands, tick- ets in hand, ready to be "processed" in ways the agents had promised. These involved being put up under rudimentary conditions on Veddel Island in the Elbe River, being fed in mess halls, and being generally watched over until sailing day.

OPPOSITE, TOP: Obligatory medical examinations under the supervision of steamship company personnel.

OPPOSITE, BOTTOM: Under the bold motto of the Hamburg American Line, emigrants wait their turn to complete departure formalities.

TOP: A rabbi reads from a text to emigrants gathered together for perhaps their final meal ashore.

BOTTOM: A dining hall in the reception center at Bremen, the rival of Hamburg in the search for steerage passengers.

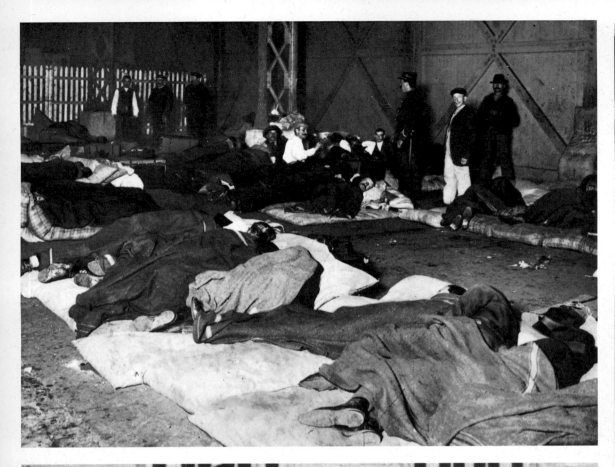

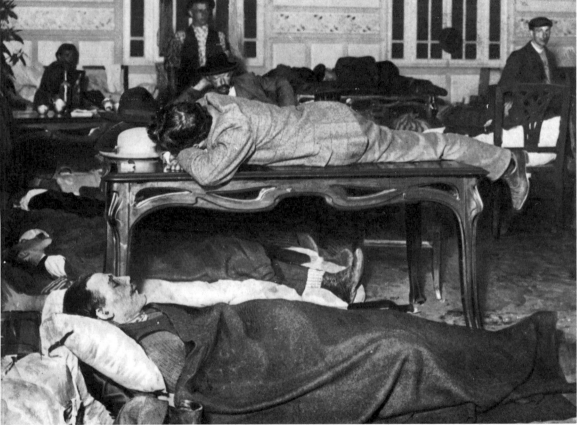

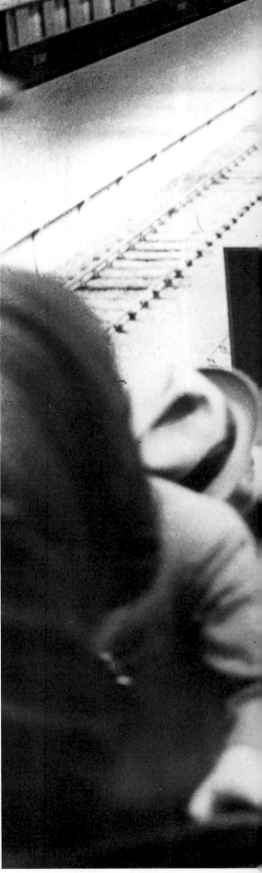

OPPOSITE: After large-scale modernization of the marine terminal in 1935, passengers arriving at Le Havre by the boat train from the Gare Saint-Lazare in Paris could board ship directly from the station platform.

ABOVE, TOP AND BOTTOM: Earlier travelers, delayed by strikes, had to spend the night on mattresses issued by steamship companies or on the Art Nouveau tables of the First Class waiting room.

OPPOSITE: Awaiting baggage from the ship before customs inspection on arrival in New York. Often delayed for as long as four hours, disembarking passengers had no recourse but to vow, as many of them did, never to travel by ship again.

ABOVE, TOP: The customs officer. One of his predecessors asked arriving Oscar Wilde the routine question "Have you anything to declare?"

"Nothing but my genius," said Wilde, and hurried to breakfast at Delmonico's.

BOTTOM: Americans on the way to *la douane* in Le Havre—when women were apt to carry as many animal skins as a Hudson Bay trapper, every well-dressed man looked like Alfred Gwynne Vanderbilt, and trunks and bags by Louis Vuitton were not status symbols but heirlooms.

OPPOSITE: Boarding the P&O's *Naldera* in 1918. Eventually, passengers would step onto gangplanks floored with rubber and protected by canvas and so pass through a tunnel without knowing just when they had become waterborne. Instead of entering the ship on lower decks, they would step into a broad reception room as busy as the lobby of a hotel catering to conventions, there to be intercepted by white-coated stewards who would relieve them of hand luggage and lead them to their cabins.

ABOVE: Embarkation, circa 1900.

TOP: Since the tidal river Thames was sometimes too shallow for liners to dock, passengers like these boarding the P&O Line's *Kyba* in 1915 would be embarked from a tender. Transatlantic travelers were not apt to board or leave their ships by tender except at Cobh, Plymouth, Cherbourg, and Gibraltar.

BOTTOM: Embarking on the *Espagne*, launched in 1909. A prototype of the vessel in Katherine Anne Porter's *Ship of Fools*, she sailed between Europe and Vera Cruz and was not scrapped until the mid-thirties.

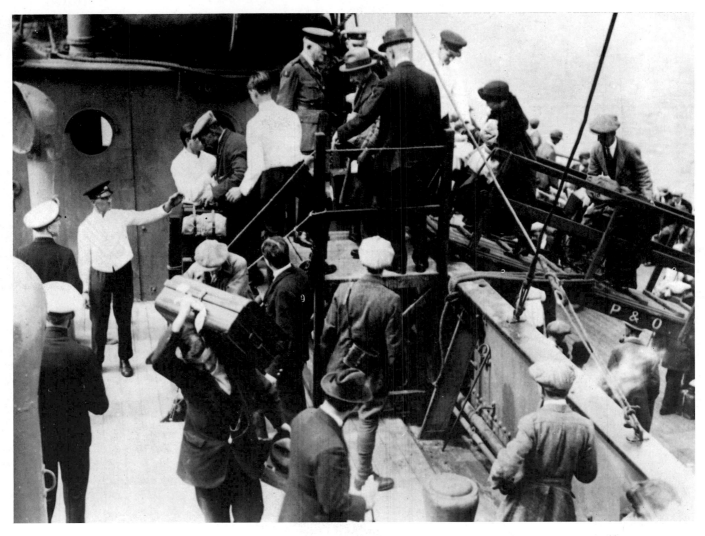

TOP: Embarkation of middle-class emigrants on the *Ballarat*, a P&O liner bound for Australia.

BOTTOM: Irish emigrants embarking for the United States in 1930 had to submit to a physical examination performed by a doctor assigned to the port of Cobh.

ABOVE: Steamer trunks loaded aboard (TOP) and taken to cabins (BOTTOM). Others that might be needed on the voyage would be placed in a special area to which passengers had access. NOT WANTED ON THE VOYAGE—a label pasted on baggage to be stored in the hold—also spelled out the title of a self-mocking romantic ballad sung by Beatrice Lillie.

OPPOSITE: Collecting luggage deposited on the deck adjacent to the *Queen Mary*'s reception hall. Many Cunard stewards were born into families in or near Southampton who had worked for the line for generations.

It was the time, wrote Lucius Beebe, "when twenty pieces of hold luggage were the absolute minimum for social survival and when even a gentleman required a wardrobe or innovation trunk in the corridor outside his stateroom to hold the four changes of clothes he was expected to make daily on an eight- or nine-day passage. They went with valets and maids, hatboxes and shoe trunks, jewel cases and, in some fastidious instances, their own personal bed linen. Invalids brought their own doctors and nurses, dog lovers traveled with mastiffs and St. Bernards. Occasional magnificoes or eccentrics brought their own barbers, and food faddists carried their special rations of sanitized lettuce leaves or graham nut bread. The transatlantic entourage of a well-placed man or woman might well number half a dozen persons, while there was no limit at all to the number of secretaries and couriers that could be kept usefully at hand. Traveling was a ritual, mannered, planned, orderly, and a matter of massive logistics. Not the least of its details was that of money."

ABOVE: A galleyway on the French Line's short-lived *Lafayette*. Launched in 1929, she was resolutely "moderne" in style, reflecting the philosophy of the company executive who asked, "Why should ladies with short skirts and bobbed hair want to sit in Louis XVI armchairs?"

OPPOSITE: A typical First Class cabin on main deck in the years when the pillaging of period styles gave way to uncluttered space, laminated surfaces, and tubular lighting.

ABOVE, TOP: The bedroom of a suite on the *Normandie*, which offered two suites with five rooms and two with six, each with its own private terrace. Located high on upper decks, these accommodations began a trend in which cabins on the main deck midship, generally the best available, were replaced by cabins on higher decks with quick access to sports decks, sun decks, and outdoor pools. As disappointed passengers would soon learn, private outdoor terraces were useless on transatlantic voyages and often on cruises because they were intolerably windy and peppered with oily soot particles.

BOTTOM: A "Pompeiian" cabin on the *France* of 1912. The proximity of the commode to the bed is a reminder of the fact that private lavatories were not considered essential to First Class comfort until well after World War I.

OPPOSITE: A passenger—or a model—in a First Class cabin on the *Paris* contemplates some hand luggage.

As the affluence of the 1920s continued to expand, hundreds of thousands of Americans found they had more money than they knew what to do with, at least in America. Among these were Scott and Zelda Fitzgerald. Contemplating a bonus of $50,000 that had come to her husband, Mrs. Fitzgerald nicely spelled out the priorities attending it. "Lustily splashing their dreams in the dark pool of gratification," she wrote,

"their fifty thousand dollars bought a cardboard day-nurse for Bonnie, a second-hand Marmon, a Picasso etching, a white satin dress . . . a dress as green as fresh wet paint, two white knickerbocker suits exactly alike, a broker's suit and two First Class tickets to Europe." At the same moment, other Americans were finding that Buick cabriolets and two-car garages, striped silk shirts and raccoon coats, "His Master's Voice" on the gramophone and Saturday on the links were no longer viable consolations. Patriotic slogans admonished good citizens to "See America First," but it was surprising how many of them wanted only to see Europe.

In some cases this urge was prompted by a sober desire to broaden one's view of the world and to see the documentations of history. In others it was an undefined hankering somehow to come to terms with that vague yet overwhelming culture whose emissaries—Bernhardt, Pavlova, Paderewski, Max Reinhardt, even voluble Queen Marie of Rumania—had made headlines from coast to coast. ("Any American with the cash and the ambition,"

said one forthright brochure, "may travel in the self-same suites occupied by these great people.") In most cases, however, Americans simply had an urge to seek fun in new surroundings and perhaps to enhance the playgrounds of the Continent with the flat sincerities of a Midwestern accent. "If you talk with Europeans," advised Julian Street, "it is always nice to give them fresh impressions of just what's the matter with their country and with them." He was addressing himself to a new breed of American traveler who, in a sense, would never go anywhere because he found no lack of advantage in where he was. This was the self-confident American yokel, the endearing ignoramus who, hearkening to the blast of the alpenhorn, had left his hay-and-seed business in northern Indiana to see more rarefied and backward parts of the world. He, said Irvin S. Cobb, was the one "who would swap any Old Master he ever saw for one peep at a set of sanitary bath fixtures."

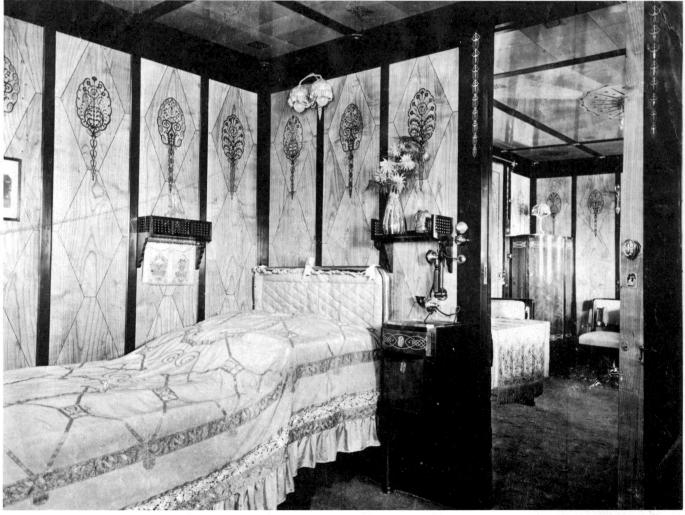

TOP: The sitting room of a luxury suite on the *Winchester Castle*. Reminiscent of Dutch interiors of the early eighteenth century, this surprising decor on a British ship was apparently chosen to appeal to the Afrikaners and ostrich-feather tycoons resident in the South African regions to which the ship sailed.

BOTTOM: A cabin on the *Bremen*—a bedroom and part of a sitting room decorated with suggestions of the Art Nouveau which, by 1912, had begun to modify some of the operatic extravagances for which German ships were known.

TOP AND BOTTOM: On board the *Ile de France*. Sitting room and dining room, separated by a wrought-iron grille, in a deluxe cabin. Incursions of emergent Art Deco upon Art Nouveau were evident in styles shown at the 1925 Exposition Internationale des Arts Décoratifs, many of whose exhibitors were commissioned to contribute interior designs for the new French Line ship.

OPPOSITE: A bathroom on the *Ile de France*, including a tub with taps for those who preferred to bathe in seawater. Bidets were essential on French ships. Shower facilities were rare on all ships until after World War II, when bathtubs, except in luxury cabins, became obsolete.

ABOVE: A bathroom on the *Felix Roussel*, 1930, the first French liner whose luxury cabins had balconies and French windows rather than portholes. The career of this twin-screw motorship reflected changing modes of sea travel: Beginning as a three-class ship with a particularly fine First Class, she ended up, nearly thirty years later, not as the two-funneled luxury ship she was meant to be but as a Swiss-owned liner with one funnel, carrying 1,000 passengers in an expanded Tourist Class and 100 in a reduced First Class, and flying the Panamanian flag.

TOP: A two-berth cabin on the *Roussillon*, built in 1906. Carrying 281 in a designated "Cabin Class" and only 26 in Third, she was a forerunner of larger and equally slow ships that would maintain the same passenger distribution.

BOTTOM: A First Class cabin on the German *Imperator*, acquired by the Cunard Line as a part of war reparations. Rechristened the *Berengaria*, she continued on the Southampton–New York run until 1938. The Pullman-like simplicity of this cabin is a reminder that even on the greatest of liners, First Class passengers were not always accommodated in tapestried opulence.

TOP: An expensive cabin on the *Viceroy of India*, launched in 1929: inlaid woodwork, curtained windows instead of portholes, brocaded furniture, and exposed plumbing.

BOTTOM: The Parisian passion for Art Nouveau extended from Métro stations to cabins on ships, like this one on the *Champollion*.

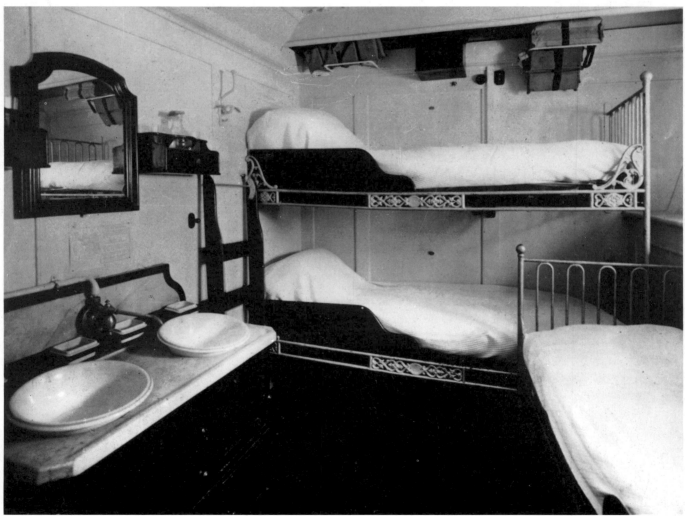

TOP AND BOTTOM: Second Class four-berth and three-berth cabins on the *Paul Lecat*, life preservers much in evidence and close at hand.

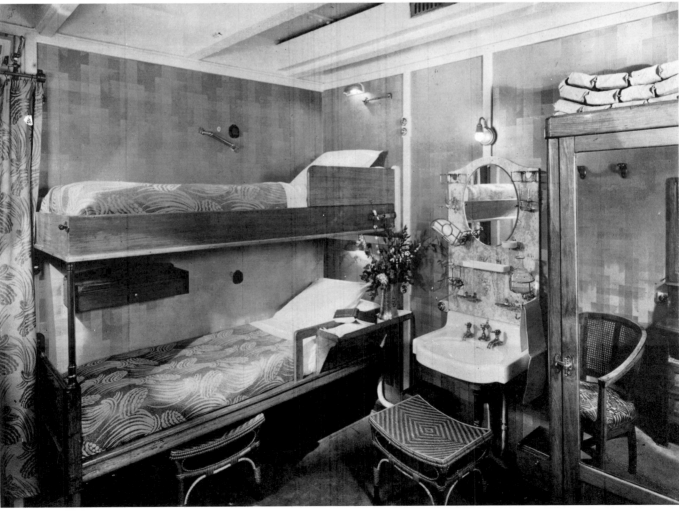

TOP: A cabin on the two-class liner *De Grasse*, one of the ships which in the era of "the five-day boat" declared herself *hors de combat* and crossed the Atlantic in a comfortable nine days.

BOTTOM: Second Class cabins on the *Paris*, which became the running mate of the *France* in 1921, were already influenced by the Art Deco that would predominate in ships of a later decade.

ABOVE TOP: A four-berth Third Class cabin on the *Chantilly*.

BOTTOM: A steerage dormitory on the French liner *Chicago*: accommodations indicating how it was possible for a ship of less than 10,000 tonnage to transport more than 1,200 emigrants and still have room for 184 passengers in Third Class and 314 in Second.

OPPOSITE: Steerage accommodations on the *Champagne*, circa 1906—the only space provided for emigrant families in which to eat and sleep. The days when emigrants slept huddled together on deck and provided their own tableware and mattresses were over, replaced now by a new day that dawned in the stench of stale vomit, unwashed bodies, and a "hearty" cuisine swilled into tin plates.

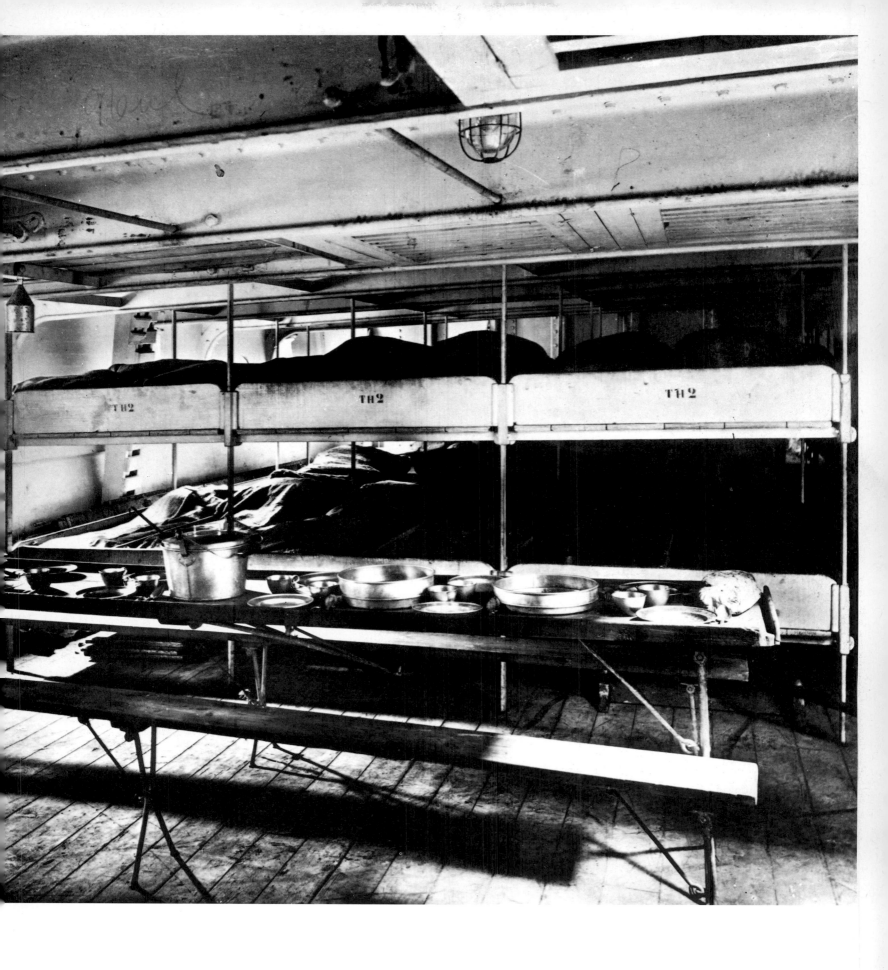

ABOVE, TOP: The First Class promenade deck on the *Chantilly*.

BOTTOM: Sailing time, 1911—extravagant millinery and velvet collars prolong *la belle époque*.

OPPOSITE: Sailing time, 1927—dropped waistlines and bobbed hair. The ship is the brand-new *Ile de France*, "boulevard of the Atlantic," preparing to sail from her New York dock.

OVERLEAF: A liner's lower depths—a descent, linked by companionways, into the infernal realm of engineers and bunker hands, low- and high-pressure boilers, oil bunkers, boiler rooms, engines, garages, baggage holds, freight storerooms, the dank hold and double bulkhead.

OPPOSITE: The stokehold of the *France*. Her 120 furnaces, fed by 206 stokers and bunker hands, burned between 750 and 800 tons of coal per day. The bunker hands delivered the coal in shovels or trolleys to the stokers, who, stripped to the waist, fed it into the furnaces. The coal then had to be spread out on the furnace grates with pokers and the slag cleared from gratings to allow air to pass. At day's end, 100 tons of cinders and ash had to be shoveled out of the furnaces and dumped into the sea.

ABOVE: The stokehold of the *Ile de France*, coal furnaces having been replaced by oil burners. Stokers now had only to watch over the burners and their supply in a working area that had lost its earlier infernal aspect.

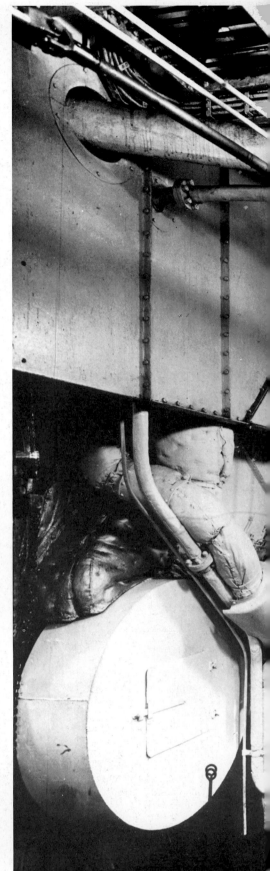

ABOVE: The Chief Engineer issues final orders before the *Ile de France* gets under way.

OPPOSITE: The stokehold of the *Normandie*. With twenty-nine main boilers and four auxiliary boilers producing steam at 62 pounds of pressure and at a temperature of 350 degrees, the ship consumed 6,500 tons of fuel per crossing. Blaise Cendrars, who crossed on her maiden voyage as correspondent for *Paris Presse*, reported: "I've just spent my first night's watch in the stokehold. I followed the progress of the fuel as it moved from level to level, I climbed ladders and threaded my way among warm bellies of huge, silvery condensers. Not a wheel or crank turned when I arrived at last in the dynamo room, and the only evidence of the invisible 164,000 horsepower that was driving and propelling the ship was the feeling of motion as it moved forward at the extraordinary speed of nearly 38 miles an hour."

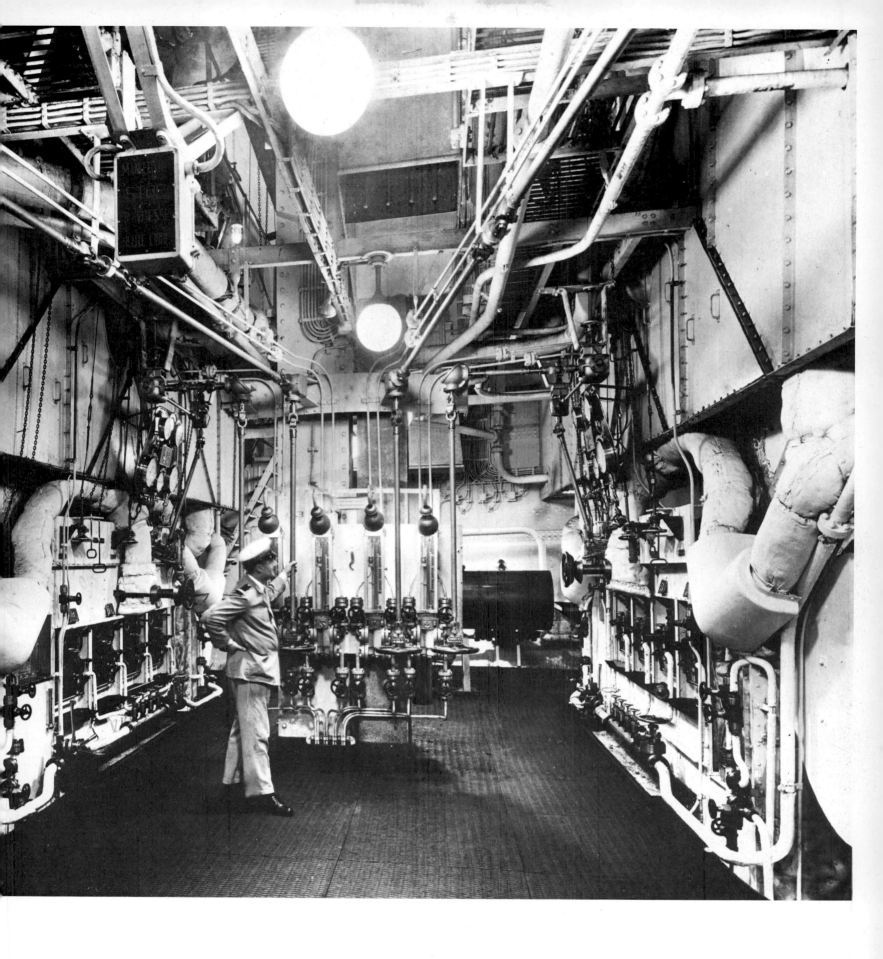

ABOVE: The watch officer at the machine room control panel, with dials enabling him to check on the functioning of all the ship's moving parts.

OPPOSITE: Aboard the *Normandie*, contact was maintained with the bridge and the central safety post by means of a 90-foot control panel. On the right are two panels controlling the screws. This installation, centralizing all remote dials and gauges of the vessel, was an early step toward automation later controlled by computer.

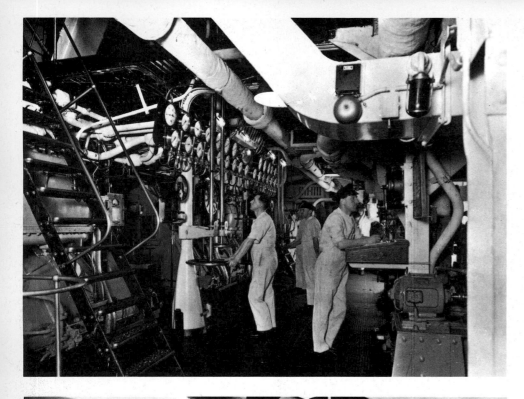

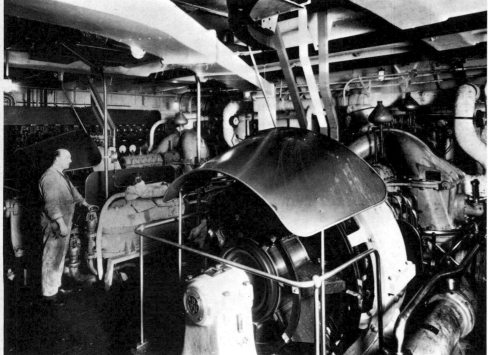

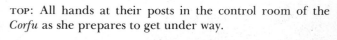

TOP: All hands at their posts in the control room of the *Corfu* as she prepares to get under way.

MIDDLE: The dynamo room on the *Stratheden*.

BOTTOM: The anchor control chamber on the *Normandie*.

OPPOSITE: The *Ormonde* leaving Sydney bound for Europe. The many-colored streamers of confetti would be held until they were snapped in two by the drift of the ship.

ABOVE: Gangplanks lowered, the *Queen Elizabeth* inches into the stream.

OPPOSITE: Mooring lines cast off, the *United States* slides backward into the Hudson. Put into service on the North Atlantic on July 3, 1952, the new flagship of the United States Line wiped out all previous speed records, crossing to Bishop's Light at a speed of 35.39 knots and permanently retiring both the mythical Blue Ribbon and the actual Blue Ribbon Trophy.

The sea lanes of the Great Circle Route after World War II belonged almost exclusively to great European liners refurbished or, as in the case of the *Queen Elizabeth*, finally given a chance to make the official maiden voyage the outbreak of war had denied them. The only American ship of any size working the Atlantic was the *America* until the new *United States* cut through the whole overdressed and overstuffed mythos of high life at sea like an eagle swooping through a flock of birds of paradise.

Aware of the power at his command, Captain Harry Manning—who had once been copilot and navigator for Amelia Earhart—began the first crossing of the *United States* modestly. But second day out, stepping up her speed to 35.6 knots—the pace of a destroyer—he saw his ship cover 801 miles, a greater distance than any other ship had ever achieved in a twenty-four-hour period. On the third day, he upped her speed to 36.17 knots, or about 41 land miles per hour. Except for Navy personnel and a few civilians, nobody knew,

and nobody would know for another sixteen years, that the *United States* could, all out, do 48 land miles per hour on a horsepower of 240,000, nearly 100,000 greater than any other liner, and that her spectacular maiden voyage, as well as every succeeding one, was made deeply under wraps.

Perhaps the most technologically sophisticated and structurally elegant of all passenger liners, the *United States* came into being by virtue of the favor and subsidy of the United States Congress. But this entailed a proviso that she be so designed as to allow her to be converted into a ship of war at a moment's notice. Interior designers did what they could to soften the austerity of a paramilitary ship, but the *United States* could not entirely disguise her origins or forget that she was enjoined always to be ready to drop her pretenses to luxury and show her naked steel.

Constructed in secrecy at Newport News from blueprints approved by the United States Navy, the *United States* had a number of "defense" fea-

tures similar to those of warships: an abnormally large fuel capacity, subdivisions of watertight compartments, and a distribution of machinery that would allow for operation of the ship even though she might be partially demolished. Should the occasion arise, she would be prepared to carry 14,000 troops a distance of 10,000 miles without stopping for fuel or water.

Only two-thirds the size of the British *Queens*, she could carry as many passengers as either of them. At 917 feet long and 102 feet abeam, she was slim enough to squeeze, if she had to, through the Panama Canal. Except for the pianos in her lounges and the butcher blocks in her kitchens, nothing on the *United States* was inflammable, including bedspreads and draperies spun of glass. The first big ship to be fireproof, she was also the first to be air-conditioned throughout.

The least "decorated" of all liners in her class, she had the functional

(*continued on following page*)

(*continued from preceding page*)

grace of a clipper ship; huge tear-shaped funnels sampan-topped; a cleanness of line and a cool shine of surface, mostly aluminum, that set her apart. Americans took to her, but Europeans did not—perhaps because she was neither *gemütlich* in feeling nor Theban in proportion, but sleek, fast, and as efficiently staffed as a midcity hotel. But while traveling Americans filled her staterooms, Americans on the whole never granted their greatest ship her title to excellence or a place among the artifacts of Yankee genius. The American public, like the European, had been living too long in the legends of floating palaces and the magical disguises of essential shipness they represented. Instead of hiding her nautical character, the *United States* exposed it; perhaps in no other vessel did all the silvery articulations of a dynamo and its agents of power so visibly obtrude. "Well, why not?" said her designer, William Francis Gibbs. "The *United States* is a ship, not an ancient inn with oaken beams and plaster walls." For all its visibility, the functional engineering of the *United States* was of a level of craft so exquisite that it threatened to dissolve the barriers separating practical art from the graphic. To sail in her was to be an involved witness to the workings of a superb machine that made quite clear its disdain for sybaritic human preferences and the venial hedonism of human habits.

118

OPPOSITE, TOP: The motorship *Georgic*, one of the last White Star liners (the company merged with Cunard in 1934), arriving at Liverpool.

BOTTOM: The *Paris* puts to sea.

ABOVE: The *Normandie* in harbor waters. The *Queen Mary* and the *Norman-die*, close contemporaries, were often compared, item by item, in regard to their appointments, with preferences made largely in terms of taste. But according to a Danish observer, the difference between them could be simply stated. "The French built a beautiful hotel and put a ship around it," he said. "The British built a beautiful ship and put a hotel inside her."

CROSSING

The bakery aboard the *Liberté*: baguettes, brioches, croissants,
prepared in the early-morning hours to be served, still warm,
for breakfast.

OPPOSITE: A mammoth wave photographed (on the third of the five *Bremens*) in January 1926, during a westward crossing. Lesser waves have been known to sweep passengers from open decks and to reach up to smash windows on the bridges of even the largest ships.

ABOVE: Captain Lévêque and his officers on the *Liberté*. This originally German ship made her maiden voyage under the French Line's flag from Le Havre on August 17, 1950, bound for New York.

OVERLEAF, LEFT: The telephone switchboard on the *Normandie*, a "miracle of technology," located next to the post and telegraph offices and the printshop.

RIGHT: Oxygen tanks on the *Normandie* were inspected regularly, as were a thousand alarm systems, hundreds of bells, and firefighting equipment.

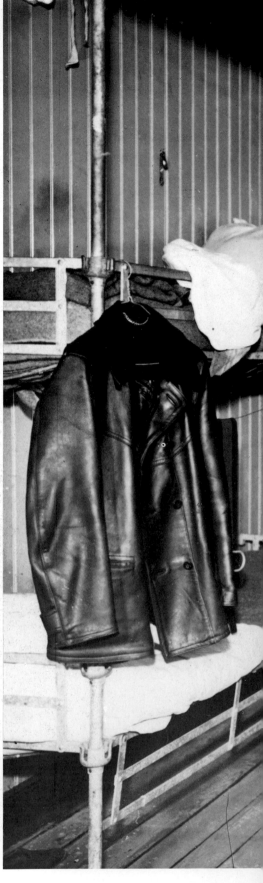

The *Normandie* was compartmentalized throughout with fire doors. Maximum use was made of nonflammable materials: marble, glass, lacquer, stucco. Combustible substances were protected with insulation and fireproofing. Fire extinguishers, both fixed and portable, were installed throughout the ship, filled with carbonic gas in the holds, foam in the boiler rooms. All the firefighting equipment was connected by telephone to a central safety station. Time would make this fact, and all other facts pertaining to fire protection on the *Normandie*, reverberate with irony.

OPPOSITE: The bridge of a Cunarder—the helmsman (*center*) stands at the controls. To his right, a sailor detailed to transmit orders to the engine room. To his left, at the window, the officer of the watch.

ABOVE, TOP: The printshop on the *Ile de France* issued a daily paper, *The Atlantic*, including news items received by radio, the day's social program, announcements of coming attractions, and menus for the day. The container for potatoes (*lower right*) was apparently a makeshift wastebasket.

BOTTOM: The *Liberté*'s radio room, an upgrading of the flimsy "shacks" erected on open decks in which wireless operators had to work until fairly late in the century.

The *Normandie* had a ship's complement of 3,117. Of this, 64 officers and crew and 700 hotel employees—managers, stewards, maîtres d'hôtel, cabin boys, maids, valets, pages, telephone operators, accountants, hairdressers—saw to the running of the ship and the comfort of passengers.

OPPOSITE: The administration office.

ABOVE: Far forward on a lower deck, postal workers sorting mail during an eastward voyage, with packets of envelopes marked "Paris Ville."

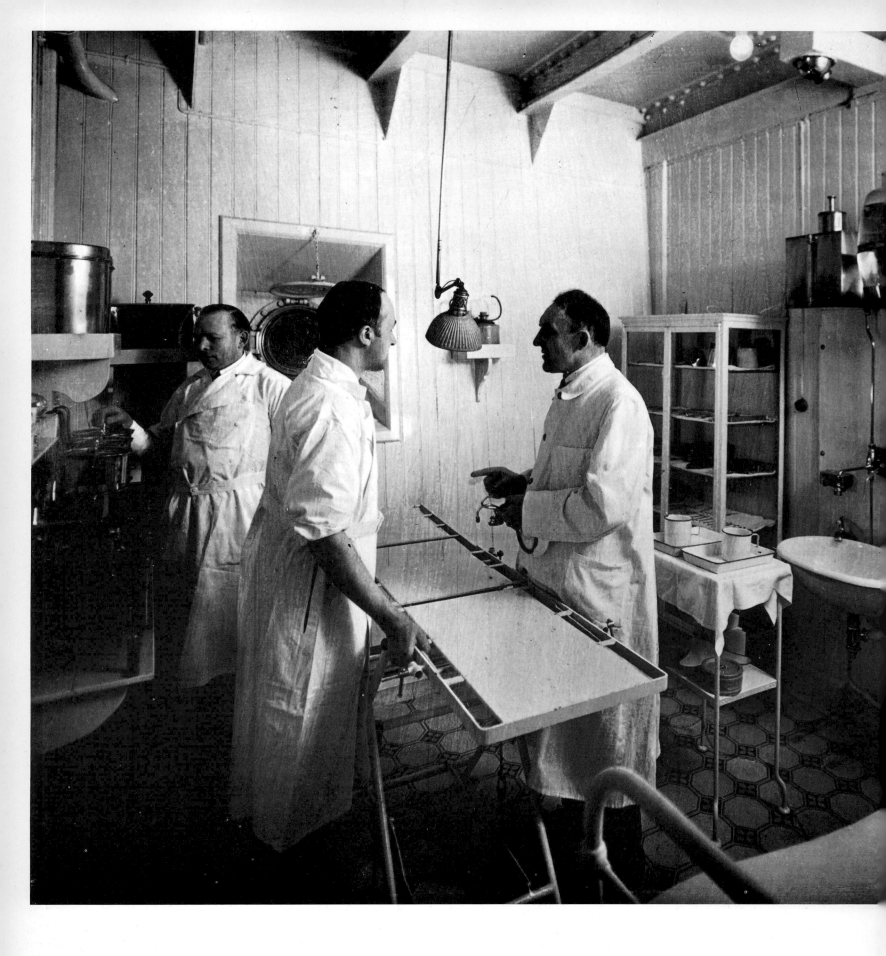

On the *Ile de France*, a hospital equipped with an operating table, a pharmacy, and an infirmary. Except on the largest of ships, surgeons, like chaplains, were often landsmen invited to contribute their services in exchange for a free crossing or a seagoing vacation. Office hours were posted; fees for services were charged.

OPPOSITE: Stewards preparing trays for delivery to cabins in the central kitchen. On ships of later vintage, breakfast and light meals were prepared by stewards in small electric kitchens on each passenger deck.

ABOVE, TOP AND BOTTOM: Walking passengers' dogs. Until the 1920s, pets were cared for by the ship's butcher, but from then on were handed over to "specialists." On the *Ile de France*, there were both a lamppost for *les chiens du boulevard* and an American-style fire hydrant. Regulations banning pets from public rooms were rigorously observed; regulations banning them from cabins, especially if the cabins were deluxe, were often "negotiable."

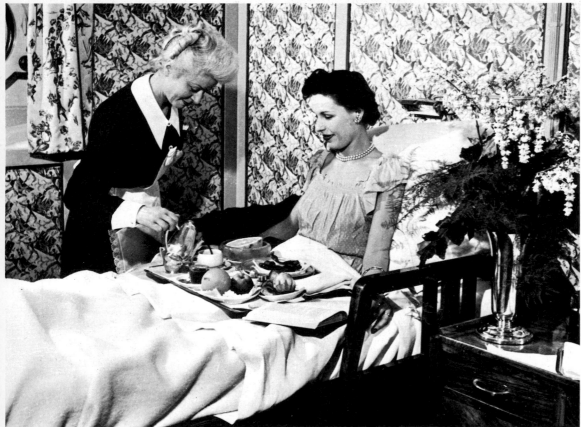

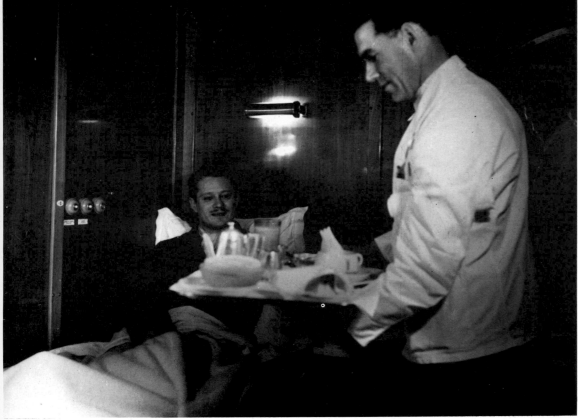

ABOVE, TOP: Breakfast in bed, served to either an uninstructed model or a passenger who slept in earrings, pearls, rings, and bracelets.

BOTTOM AND OPPOSITE: Until the late years of the steamship era, only stewards served single male passengers, only stewardesses female passengers, while couples were taken care of by both.

Service staffs on British and French liners tended to be efficient and reserved to the point of sullenness; On Italian liners one of the distinctive features of life at sea was the bemused demeanor of their crews and the pervasive sense of domestic intimacy this assured. Zest for a good table and the white-linen amenities of the nineteenth century gave even the most modern of Italian ships a combined air of opulence and

hominess; and a characteristic open curiosity about everything human on the part of their staffs nicely checked the pretensions to aristocratic elegance the Italian Line's advertising encouraged. Unlike workers on vessels conceived in northern weather and Lutheran sobriety, the Neopolitans and Genovese who accepted the disciplines necessary to the workings of a great liner were not repressed by them. The ageless stewardesses of the Cunard ships, with their flat shoes and flat faces, often looked as though they might have been in the Crimea with Florence Nightingale. On an Italian ship, a passenger pressing his call button would likely be greeted in a few moments by a stand-in for Sophia Loren. As she stood poised on the threshold of his cabin, costumed in black skin-tight poplin and frills of a sort once associated only with postcards depicting the raunchier side of domestic life in Paris, his signorina would address him with one enormously self-assured stare. "Sir," she would ask, "what can I do for you?"

ABOVE: The lower part of the two-level boat deck of the *Pasteur*, later the last of the five German ships named *Bremen* and easily identified at a distance by a single funnel far forward.

OPPOSITE: In the absence of deck chairs, Third Class *Ile de France* passengers occupy a bench of a sort that did not disappear until Third Class became Tourist Class and, in terms of space, the dominant accommodation on many of the last ships to offer transatlantic service.

Any volume illustrating the final decades of transatlantic ship travel must, perforce, be concerned with images of mechanical power and aesthetic aspirations, with those whose skills ensured the operation of the one and those whose means and appetites encouraged the other. In the interests of technology and social history, that emphasis is natural. But in terms of sociology, it obscures an unignorable fact: Of the millions of souls who boarded ships in the heyday of ships, four out of five crossed the ocean in conditions ranging steeply downward from the austere to the wretched. Some examples of austerity are pictured here. But bare clean dormitories and deck scenes suggesting a cozy degree of social intercourse or an atmosphere of picnic joviality disguise a reality that was unspeakable. Emigrant quarters—the steerage on British ships, the *entrepont* on French—were vomitoriums in which, often, as many as a hundred people had access to but one toilet. Sleeping accommodations were verminous mattresses, mealtime a call to line up with tin plates for

portions of gruel and versions of *olla podrida* ladled out of iron vats. When these quarters were battened down against bad weather, sometimes for days on end, human effluvia made them stench holes. When they were open, emigrants with the strength to do so might find a place on deck far forward or far aft, but only to huddle among winch engines and oily hawsers. Photographically, this seam of ocean transport would be about as interesting and just as numbing as a thousand shots of the wooden tables and bunkhouse walls of Stalag 17.

OPPOSITE, BOTTOM: A family of Scottish emigrants en route to Canada around 1911.

TOP AND ABOVE: As late as 1935, emigrants leaving Germany for South America were subject to conditions once associated only with the word "steerage."

OVERLEAF, LEFT: 1907. One of the most famous photographs of this century: emigrants photographed by Alfred Stieglitz aboard the *Kaiser Wilhelm II*.

RIGHT: Deck sports for Third Class passengers on the *Empress of Britain*, 1911, sailing regularly between Liverpool and Montreal.

ABOVE, TOP: The extraordinary swimming pool of the *Viceroy of India*, launched in 1929.

BOTTOM: The pool of the *Aquitania*, which made a first transatlantic crossing in June 1914.

OPPOSITE: The first oceangoing swimming pool to be built in a giant liner, that of the *Imperator*, 1913.

TOP: The open-air pool on the *De Grasse*.

BOTTOM: Crossing the equator (on the *Mongolia*, P&O Line, in September 1933)—an occasion often marked by baptismal rites for those passengers crossing the line for the first time. Fully clothed, they were expected to submit to dunking in the ship's pool, which was often no more than a large canvas bag, and to join the attendant merriment presided over by Neptune and, sometimes, Amphitrite.

TOP AND BOTTOM: On the *Normandie*, the 75-foot First Class swimming pool, equipped with a bar, was lined with 380,000 Sèvres blue and white enameled porcelain tiles. Space at the shallow end was reserved for children and otherwise open to passengers, or models, in street clothing.

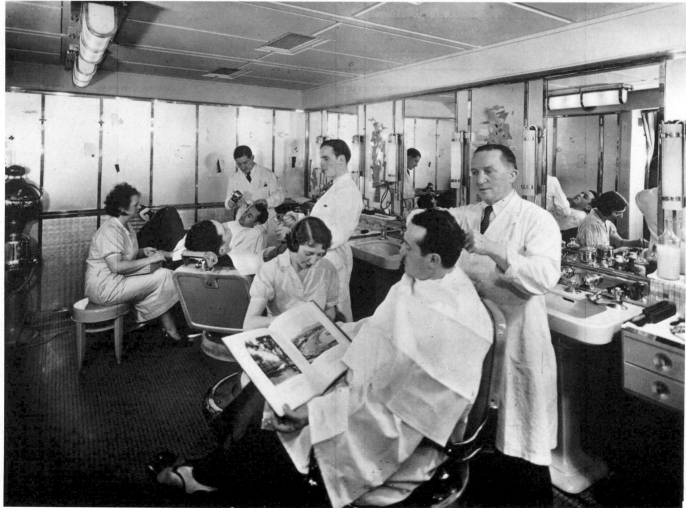

TOP AND BOTTOM: The women's and men's hairdressing salons
on the *Normandie*.

TOP: The *Normandie*'s sinister infirmary and dentist's office.

BOTTOM: The *Queen Mary*'s *sauna pour dames*.

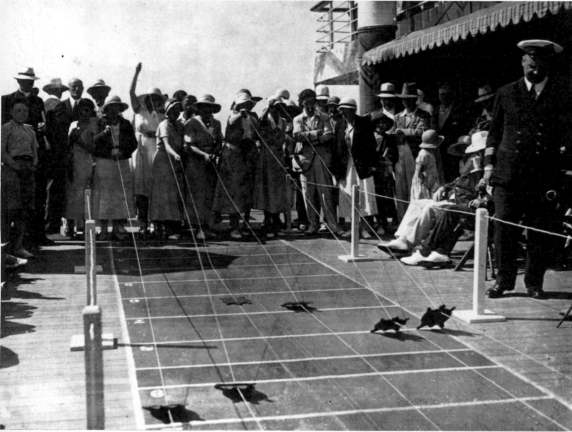

TOP: Tug-of-war, a popular shipboard pastime in the 1930s.

BOTTOM: Cardboard piglets in sundeck competition. Aboard ship, people will bet on anything, a propensity profitably channeled in later years by the widespread installation of gaming rooms afloat offering roulette, craps, blackjack, and slot machines. Among the employees of the *Queen Elizabeth 2* are two men whose sole function it is to see that all the one-armed bandits are in good working order.

OPPOSITE: Between funnels on the *Normandie*, a midocean tennis match. Only a very few other ships had sufficient open deck space to make this possible; and since the bounding main posed hazards not encountered at Wimbledon or Forest Hills, tennis at sea was not taken seriously, except by the producers of French Line brochures.

TOP: Deck tennis, in high heels.

BOTTOM: Shuffleboard players, apparently unaware that disks must be assembled before the game can continue.

297 LE HAVRE. — Le Transatlantique "France". — Le Bowling. — LL.

TOP AND BOTTOM: Skeet shooting, ring toss, Ping-Pong, bowling: First Class passengers could indulge in them all.

OPPOSITE: Dispensing with chair pads, some of the *Queen Mary*'s crew take a moment in the sun outside the Verandah Grill. Required to be qualified sailors, officers were also expected to possess manners and sophistication in worldly matters equal to those of their passengers, and, if that were the case, to conceal the fact.

ABOVE: A language lesson, putting first things first. Since a majority of passengers was American, French Line personnel were expected to know a bit of English.

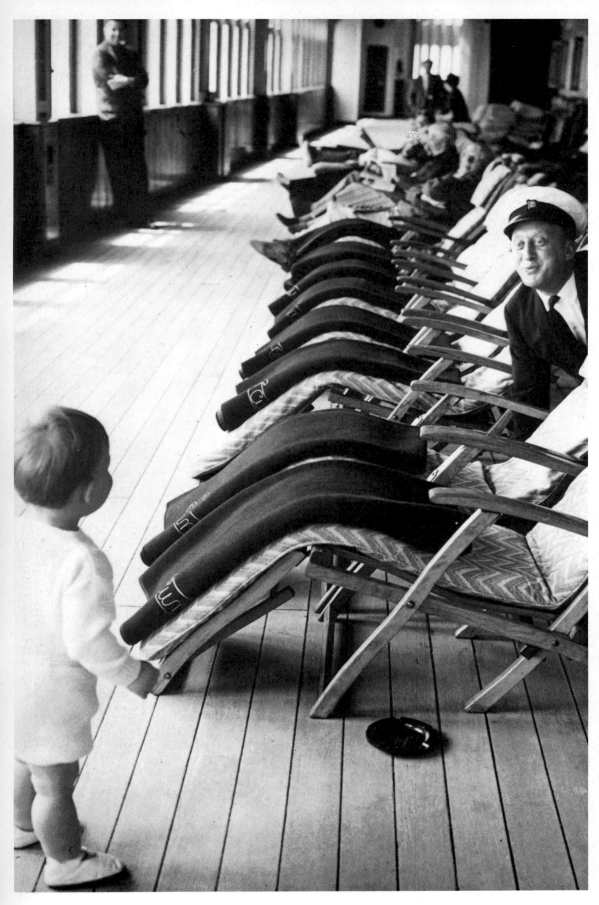

ABOVE: Far forward on the *Queen Mary*'s enclosed promenade deck, an encounter.

OPPOSITE: Tea time. French ships, every ship, made the British custom *de rigueur*. Here, the Chief Deck Steward and two assistants serve bare plates and pots of air to models pretending to be passengers.

ABOVE: From the laying of the keel to the launching, the building of ships has always been an activity involving far more than the skills of shipwrights. When vessels with painted eyes and animal heads walked on the water like enormous centipedes, their characters were immediately visible, and their purposes. Eventually, animistic signs gave way to the mythic and homuncular; ships came to bear figureheads representing everything from bare-breasted divinities and barbaric queens to Toby-jug uncles and demure maiden aunts in mobcaps. In every case, these were manifestations of the belief that ships were more than mere artifacts, that they shared animal nature with beasts of prey and human nature with warriors, traders, and those who kept the home fires burning.

The last notably antiquarian symbol on the Atlantic Ocean was the eagle on the prow of the *Imperator*, which, launched in 1913, was capable, fully booked, of carrying nearly 5,500 souls, a figure ships of later decades would not even remotely approach. This bland-eyed bird, crudely grotesque and ugly as sin, was installed as much for the purpose of increasing the length of the ship as for tribal reasons. With a dinky little crown on its snakelike head, it rode the waves only until the *Imperator*'s third voyage, when an angry sea

reached up, ripped the whole business from the prow, and drowned it. Twenty-five years later, when the *Imperator*, rechristened *Berengaria*, was retired, ships were apt to be identified not so much by what they showed outside as by what they carried inside. Eclecticism was curbed by then, history's bandboxes and attics thoroughly rifled. Instead of castles on the Rhine, or royal hunting lodges, or unconscious parodies of the Stately Home, ships were becoming fairly tasteful museums of arts and crafts indigenous to their countries of origin. The grandiose having reached the otiose, a new dispensation made room for things as modest as Navajo sand paintings on the *United States*; decorative examples of wood like zebrano, coromandel, Australian bean, padauk, thuya, and primavera from the reaches of the Empire on the *Queen Elizabeth*; and on the *Leonardo da Vinci* reproductions of the inventions and drawings of her namesake. One of the most beautiful of these museum representations was the Britannia dining room of the *Queen Elizabeth 2*, in which all the swagger and panache of Nelsonian scarlet, brass, and navy blue dressed a bright space where exquisite models of early Cunarders placed in glass were visible from four sides. But, like so much else on that ship, this room was dismantled and redone, to be replaced by a kitschy warren called "Restaurants of the World" undistinguishable from the pagodas and coachhouse restaurants found in suburban shopping centers.

ABOVE: *Rauchzimmer* to smoking room. In her British reincarnation after World War I, the *Imperator* as the *Berengaria* was still identified by the Teutonic weightiness that gave rise to the term "Berengaria Baroque."

ABOVE, TOP: The winter garden of the *Normandie*, complete with fountains and aviaries.

BOTTOM: The *France's* Moorish saloon, a holdover from the days when every well-appointed home had a "Turkish corner."

OPPOSITE, TOP: A verandah café on Cunard's *Laconia*, circa 1930.

BOTTOM: The *Viceroy of India's* appropriately decorated verandah café.

162

OVERLEAF: The *Viceroy of India*'s First Class reading and writing room (*left*), complete with fake fireplace and the hassocks and pillows the British call poufs, and the same ship's smoking room (*right*), baronial and Scottish. Both of these rooms are now settings only for marine life off the North African coast of Oran where, on November 11, 1942, the *Viceroy of India* was torpedoed by Nazi Unterseeboot-407.

SECOND OVERLEAF: The main saloon of the *Imperator*: a helmeted bust of Kaiser Wilhelm (and electric fan) in the background, Germans and Americans in the foreground.

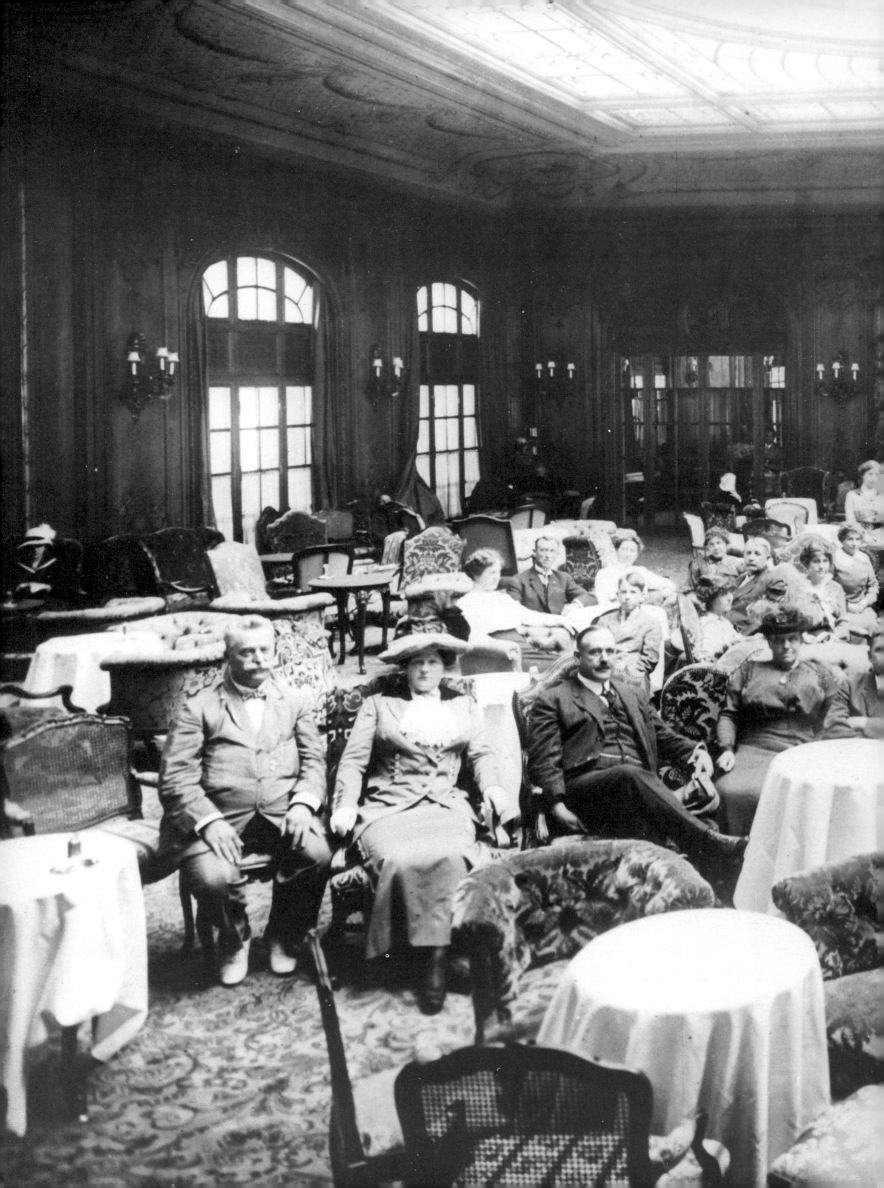

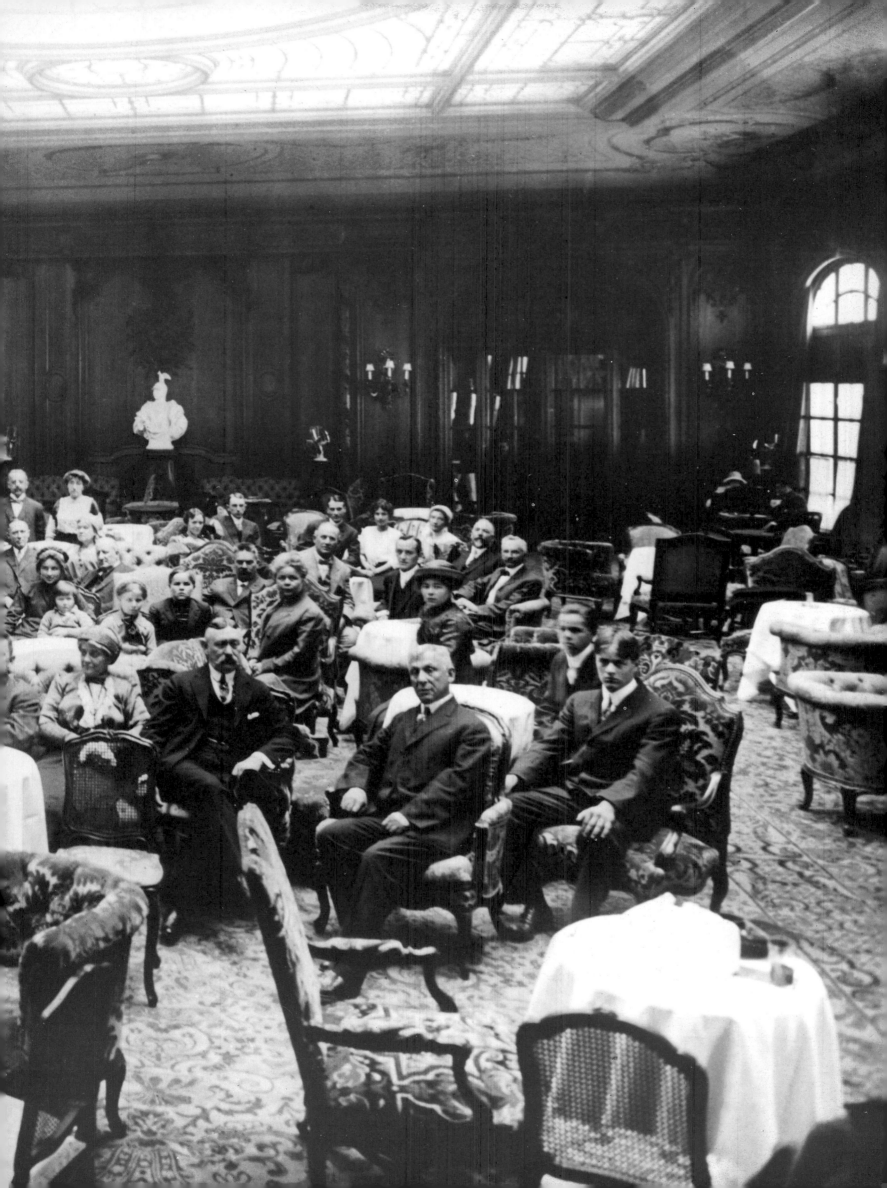

PRECEDING PAGES, LEFT: The smoking saloon and bar, Dutch tiles providing the central motif. To the left of the chimneypiece is a reproduction of the reproduction of the Round Table of King Arthur hanging in the *actual* Winchester Castle.
RIGHT: A corner of the First Class saloon of the *Winchester Castle*.

ABOVE, TOP: Another view of the First Class saloon of the *Winchester Castle*.

BOTTOM: Transformed into a ballroom, the grand saloon of the *Imperator* with an example of the glass-domed ceilings familiar on German ships since late in the nineteenth century.

ABOVE, TOP: The librarian hands books to a model posing as a passenger.

BOTTOM: On the bridge of the *Ile de France*, Captain Franck Garrigue with the French actor Victor Francen—the prototype of thousands of photographs in which transatlantic skippers stand beside business tycoons, public officials, sports figures, and entertainers.

ABOVE: The corridor off the *Aquitania*'s grand saloon.

OPPOSITE: The 1912 *France*, advertised as "The Versailles of the Atlantic," or "the floating chateau." Her *salon de conversation* was supposed to bring back the causerie of royal residences under the encouragement of gilded white paneling, armchairs upholstered with Aubusson tapestry, royal blue carpetings, and coffered ceiling, along with copies of paintings of the Sun King at either end (one based on Hyacinthe Rigaud's full-length portrait and the other on Van der Meulen's painting of the king after the hunt).

No one can be sure just when, or on what particular ship, the operatic and gargantuan phase of interior decoration on transatlantic liners first showed the aesthetic temper that would set a mode. But a good case could be made for the decor of the Norddeutscher Lloyd's *Lahn* once the designer Johannes Poppe of Bremen was done with her. Put into service as early as 1887, the *Lahn* had been designed so that her richly bedighted interiors would represent no less than "a glittering robe . . . to cover enforced exigencies." In other words, the business of hiding the "shippy" character of a ship under alien trappings of swag and filigree had begun.

When the little *Lahn*, of barely 6,000 tonnage, came onto the ocean scene loaded like a cathedral with arches and mosaics, gilded railings, allegorical statues, and cherubs blowing into golden trumpets, the age of magnificence—under the auspices of the German Empire—had been launched. German ships in the following years would become temples of high baroque, grand galleries of an aspiration so Valkyrian that one would think only megalomaniacs might dally there. Before long, the lambency of emergent Art Nouveau would begin to restrain the Teutonic apostles of giantism and curb their displays of eclectic incontinence. But up to the outbreak of World War I, German marine decor would command interest combining admiration with ridicule, and envy with secret desires on the part of non-German designers for emulation. Given its historical period and the perspective from which we view it now, this kind of art for the affluent at sea reflected a world that was moribund and doomed. Part Richard Wagner, part Victor Herbert, its harmonies were nevertheless sufficiently viable to juxtapose the classic with the kitsch in a symphony of uncertain taste wholly appropriate to its audience.

TOP: Shops at sea provided passengers with diversion and a nonessential selection of goods. The commercialism they introduced to ocean travel was at first confined to specific deck areas that could be visited at will. But as shipboard shopping became big business, ships began to take on the aspect of floating bazaars. When merchandisers were joined by advertisers, the gradual triumph of cold cash over decorative design was unignorable.

In the last years of the *Queen Elizabeth*, the great promenade deck foyer was still a place of rendezvous and, like a city square, a crossroads; but passengers passing through or gathering there had to stay clear of signboards six feet high flanking a shiny Hillman-Minx which could be purchased on the spot from a sea-going salesman.

On the *France*, the triumph was exquisite: Little grottoes placed throughout the ship, which might have housed figurines of saints or mythological deities, housed instead ingenious bottles from the *parfumeurs* of the Rue Saint-Honoré. The fact that these and their display settings showed a far higher level of taste and craftsmanship than anything else on the ship did not go unremarked.

What the designers had in mind for the entrance foyer of the *Queen Elizabeth 2* was a room of low-keyed elegance with a dropped-level circle of banquettes in the center of which was to be placed a Henry Moore sculpture, or one of Barbara Hepworth's delicate constructions, and around the black velvet walls of which would be placed still other examples of contemporary British genius. What they got was neither Hepworth nor Moore nor any other manifestation of British genius except illuminated advertisements for Schweppes tonic water and Rothman cigarettes.

MIDDLE: By 1936, when shipboard classes were designated First, Cabin, Tourist, even the least of these offered public rooms of a style and comfort equal to those found only in First Class at the turn of the century.

BOTTOM: The First Class observation lounge of the *Queen Mary* as it originally appeared. In the mid-sixties, this room was given over to Tourist Class and its decoration to the whimsies of bartenders. A. A. Thompson's famous mural painting, *The Royal Jubilee Week, 1935*, then had to compete for attention with papier-mâché shamrocks, dolls in national costumes, stuffed animals, and colored postcards from the boardwalk at Bournemouth and the pier at Brighton.

OPPOSITE: The *Queen Mary*'s main lounge—Art Deco of proportions close to those of the Radio City Music Hall, extending upward through three deck levels.

174

TOP: In the Second Class lounge of the *Stratheden*, models play checkers and piano.

BOTTOM: The chapel of the *Ile de France*—the crucifixion in pressed glass; the two patron saints of France, St. Genevieve and Joan of Arc, in stained-glass windows.

TOP: The living room of a suite on the *Paris*.

BOTTOM: The Art Deco writing room of the *Ile de France*.

Children were provided with everything from sand boxes to carousels; entertained with Punch and Judy shows; watched over by trained nurses; invited to costume parties. Some ships scheduled special dinner hours for them, installed bathing pools and soda fountains for them, and otherwise tried to keep them out of sight and out of lounge bars. Adolescents, for

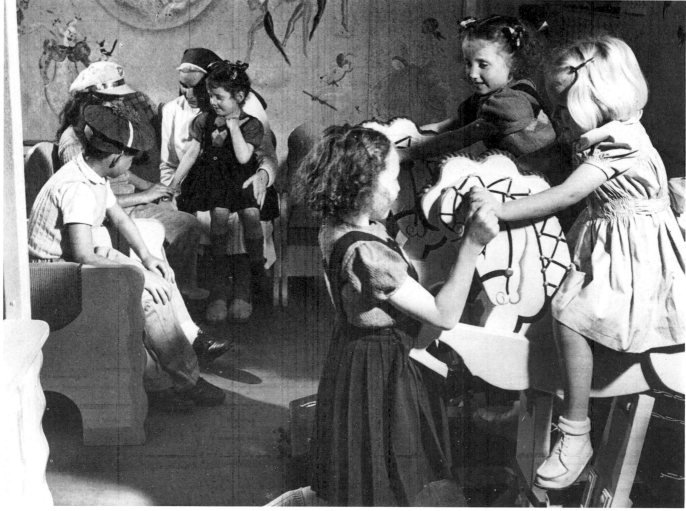

decades the lost souls of an Atlantic crossing, did not come into their own until the last years of the steamship era when dis-cothèques with soft drink bars, situated in remote parts of ships, served them as hangouts.

OPPOSITE: The central kitchen on the *Normandie*, with 200 feet of electric stoves and three 55-foot ovens. Seventy-six chefs and more than a hundred assistants turned out some 4,000 meals every day. There was also a smaller kitchen serving the grill room and another for the preparation of kosher food.

ABOVE, TOP: Dishwashers, electric and human.

BOTTOM: The potato peeler.

OVERLEAF: In the kitchens of the *France*, a team of cooks works around one of the huge stainless-steel stoves, all of which had guard-rail edges that could be quickly raised in the event of rough weather.

Kitchen staffs, headed by a master chef, included a roasting chef, a chef *saucier*, a fry chef, and one responsible for hors d'oeuvres.

TOP: Monsieur Vigne in the *Liberté*'s kitchen, opening cans of caviar of which, on a round-trip voyage, 175 to 250 pounds would be consumed.

BOTTOM: The Gallic diffidence of Chef Magrin.

OPPOSITE, TOP: Too many cooks, put to the test.

BOTTOM: Roasts, skewered and crowned.

OPPOSITE: Pastries ready for the dining room. The candy ribbons and bows, along with swans and unicorns modeled in ice, were likely to turn up at the midnight buffet.

ABOVE, TOP: Aboard the *Liberté*, hors d'oeuvres.

BOTTOM: The pastry chef presents his witch's cottage.

TOP: *Queen Mary* stewards give a final touch to uniforms.

MIDDLE: The Tourist Class ironing room on the *Stratheden*, 1937. A boon to less-than-affluent passengers, this facility was also a fire hazard.

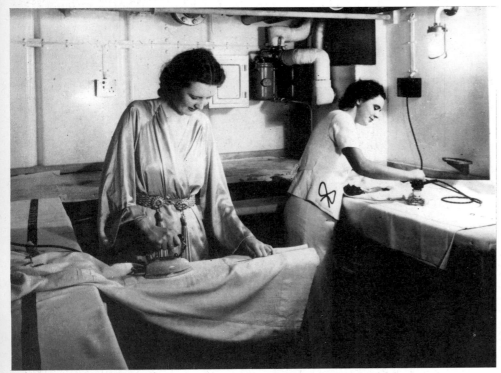

BOTTOM AND OPPOSITE: For dinner, black tie and formal gowns were the rule on liners, but only in First Class. In later years, the day's printed program would carry a "Suggested Dress" notice which, in practice, applied only to men. Women continued to wear evening gowns long after their husbands, ticketed to make the return trip by air, refused to lug evening clothes around Europe simply to satisfy the expectations of shipboard custom.

TOP: On the *Felix Roussel*, designer Paul Lecat's elevator might have been removed intact from a Parisian hotel.

MIDDLE: The *Normandie*'s eleven decks were connected by twenty-three elevators and dumbwaiters. Here, the cage of one with a metalwork motif of gilded seashells.

BOTTOM: The *Champollion*'s elevator led to an Egyptian rendezvous.

OPPOSITE: Entrance hall and grand staircase of the *Ile de France*.

OVERLEAF: The stairs to the dining room of the *Cordillière*, 1895 (LEFT), and the *Deutschland*'s dining room (RIGHT). By a few years, these preceded in seating arrangements, if not in grandeur, the saloons in which tables for four to eight people were most numerous; and, by many years, the introduction of tables for two.

Launched in 1900, the *Deutschland* was one of a fleet of German ships that succeeded in maintaining precedence over British ships for a period of nearly ten years. Correctly sensing that the ornate and outsize would appeal to the affluent far more than British shipboard "coziness," her owners gave both architect and decorator a free hand. While the British aimed for public rooms that would be "silent sermons in good taste," the Germans reached for the sky. Expanding on dining rooms like the one pictured here, marine architects saw to it that the dining room on the *Kaiser Wilhelm* would rise through three stories, the one on the *Kronprinzessin Cecilie* through four.

As decorators on these ships did up bedrooms with "pale stripes of gold-tinted blue—the combination . . . borrowed from peacock feathers—otherwise decorated all in white, whilst the walls and furniture of the adjoining parlor were covered with silvery leather," even luxury accommodations on British ships began to seem as drab as the "bed-sits" of the Bayswater Road.

The British, caustic about frivolity on sea lanes established by cheese-paring Samuel Cunard and long kept "sensible" by his heirs, had still to countenance another innovation of the Hamburg American Line—big fish tanks on "awning decks" which allowed passengers to catch their own carp, pike, tench, and trout and have them cooked to order that evening.

Total emulation of what they derided would not occur for years, but the British made a start by matching the number of funnels on the new express German liners. The *Deutschland* had four, as did her immediate successors, so placed as to make two pairs, fore and aft. In the mind of the public, these came to stand for ultimate marine power and safety, and there were instances where agents soliciting emigrants could not talk their potential clients into sailing on a ship with any fewer. The British placed their funnels equidistant, but four was the number visible on every large Cunard or White Star ship until the *Aquitania* and the *Britannic* ended such redundant shows of power in 1914.

PRECEDING PAGES, LEFT: The dining room aboard the *France*, where, for the first time, comparatively small tables were available. Its 25-foot ceiling and grand staircase were copies of those in the townhouse of the Comte de Toulouse.

RIGHT: The wrought-iron and glass dining room of the *Paris,* two stories high. In the foreground is the railing of the grand staircase; in the background, a fresco by Albert Besnard. Designers in the first decades of the century, ignoring the explosions of Fauvist and Cubist art they must have heard, stayed with the academic and safe products of bourgeois taste.

TOP: The Second Class dining room on the *Viceroy of India*.

MIDDLE: The Ritz-Carlton restaurant on the *Imperator*, where service was *à la carte*. With this innovation the traveler could now buy his ticket marked "With Meals" or "Without Meals." If he chose the latter he would dine in the Ritz-Carlton, where "it may be taken for granted that a brigade of chefs trained by Escoffier and a brigade of waiters trained by Ritz made the cuisine and service as renowned as that of the famous restaurants ashore."

Allowing for dining at no fixed time and no *prix fixe*, this new arrangement pleased a sufficient number of First Class passengers to allow for its continuance to the very end of the steamship era. By that time, the old sense of honor that had attended an invitation to dine at the Captain's Table had been replaced by the sense of affluence that directed passengers to the Verandah Grill.

BOTTOM: The *Queen Mary's* dining room. Three deck levels in height, it could accommodate 800 passengers at one sitting. A large mural map over the entrance showed a small model of the ship moving in synchronization with her hour-to-hour progress.

OPPOSITE: The grand entrance. Long after the ships of other nations had given it up, French ships continued to make this possible, via red-carpeted stairs and the attentions of tip-hungry *maîtres d'*.

The *Normandie* began her maiden voyage at 4:20 P.M. on May 29, 1935; a few hours later (OVERLEAF) her passengers learned what to expect.

DINER

Hors-d'Œuvre	Olives Vertes - Olives Noires - Céleri en Branches Cantaloup frappé au Sherry Tomates Surprise - Salade Marinette - Mayonnaise de Turbot
Potages	Consommé Froid Rubis en tasse Consommé Vermicelle Consommé Belle Fermière Potage Solférino Soupe à l'Oignon
Poissons	Brochet de la Loire au Beurre Blanc Filet de Turbot Paiva
Entrée	Noix de Ris de Veau Braisée Carême
Spécialité Régionale	**Le Caneton à l'Orange**
Légumes	Haricots Verts Frais au Beurre d'Isigny Petits Pois Frais à la Française Courgettes à la Maintenon
Pommes de terre	Purée - au Four - à l'Anglaise - en Robe Pommes Nouvelles Persillées
Pâtes	Spaghetti - Nouilles - Macaroni (Gratin 10 minutes) Riz Nature - Riz au Kari
Rôtis	Poularde de Bresse à la Broche Côte de Charolais Rôtie à l'Anglaise
Buffet Froid	Jambon de Parme, - Jambon de Virginie Jambon de Prague - Jambon de Westphalie - Jambon d'York Bœuf Mode en Gelée Longe de Veau à la Gelée Printanière - Poulet Froid Carré de Porc Froid - Selle d'Agneau Sauce Menthe Côte de Bœuf Froide Terrine de Foie Gras Truffé Dindonneau Froid Cranberry Sauce Langouste Mayonnaise - Barbue Froide Sauce Antiboise
Salades	Cœur de Laitue - Panachée - Chicorée - Endives Salades de Pointes d'Asperges - Salade de Soissons
Fromages	Petit Suisse - Neufchâtel - Pont-l'Evêque Roquefort - Hollande - Emmenthal
Pâtisserie	Gâteau Ananas Espagnolettes - Langues
Entremets	Crème Viennoise - Bavaroise Framinée Pudding Choiseul
Glaces	Vanille - Pistache - Abricot - Melon Bombe Impériale
Fruits	Corbeille de Fruits Compote de Fruits Frais
Vins	Grand Vin Rouge et Blanc des Caves de la Compagnie Générale Transatlantique
Thés - Cafés, etc.	Thé de Chine - Orange Pekoë Verveine - Tilleul - Menthe - Camomille Café Américain - Café Sanka - Café Français

M E

Mercredi

Menu

Cantaloup F

Potag

Brochet de la L

Le Canet

Petits Pois F

Bomb

Corbei

S. S. "NO

DINNER

...

Green Olives - Ripe Olives - Celery	**Hors-d'Œuvre**
Iced Cantaloupe in Sherry Wine	
Tomatoes Surprise - Marinette Salad - Mayonnaise of Turbot	
Cold Consomme in Cup	**Soup**
Vermicelli Consomme	
Belle Fermière Consomme	
Solferino Soup	
Onion Soup	
Pike in Butter	**Fish**
Fillets of Turbot Paiva	
Braised Sweetbread Carême	**Entrée**
Duckling à l'Orange	**Special French Dish**
New String Beans in Isigny Butter	**Vegetables**
New Green Peas à la Française	
Pumpkins à la Maintenon	
Mashed - Baked - English Style - Boiled	**Potatoes**
Parsley Potatoes	
Spaghetti - Noodles - Macaroni (gratin 10 minutes)	**Pastes**
Rice - Indian Curry	
Poularde de Bresse à la Broche	**Roast**
Roast Rib of Charolais à l'Anglaise	
Parme Ham - Virginia Ham	**Cold Buffet**
Prager Ham - Westphalia Ham - York Ham	
Beef Mode in Jelly	
Loin of Veal Jelly Printanière - Cold Chicken	
Cold Rack of Pork - Saddle of Spring Lamb Mint Sauce	
Cold Rib of Beef	
Truffed Terrine of Foie Gras	
Cold Young Turkey Cranberry Sauce	
Rock-Lobster Mayonnaise - Cold Brill Sauce Antiboise	
Heart of Lettuce - Mixed - Chicory - Endives	**Salads**
Asparagus Tip Salad - Beans Salad	
Cream Cheese - Neufchâtel - Pont-l'Evêque	**Cheeses**
Roquefort - Dutch Cheese - Emmenthal	
Pineapple Cake	**French Pastry**
Espagnolettes - Langues	
Viennoise Cream - Bavaroise Praline	**Entremets**
Pudding Choiseul	
Vanilla - Pistachio - Apricot - Melon	**Ice Cream**
Imperial Ice Cream	
Assorted Fruits	**Fruits**
Stewed French Fruits	
Grand Vin Rouge et Blanc des Caves	**Wines**
de la C...	
China Tea - Orange Pekoe	**Tea - Coffee, etc.**
Verveine - Linden Tea - Mint - Camomile	
American Coffee - Swiss Coffee - French Coffee	

In the earliest years of scheduled crossings of the Atlantic, food provided to passengers was sometimes at the mercy of the Captain's budget, charity, or whim. In the penultimate years, one steamship company made the disastrous and short-lived innovation of offering meals *á la carte* and cafeteria-style. Between these extremes, the amounts and kinds of food available to other than steerage passengers remained curiously static for a hundred years. If a study of early-twentieth-century menus is indicative, the trencherman appetites of the nineteenth were gradually refined by cosmopolitan touches, but never curbed. Well past World War II, ships continued to serve food in portions and varieties recalling the days of Diamond Jim Brady at Delmonico's. In the paddle-wheel decades and into those of steamships with sails, the groaning board served an important function, banning ennui and promoting shipboard society at one long table. The bugle call that alerted passengers to dinnertime, and the "steamship round" of roast they could at leisure decimate, served as forms of entertainment. But even as late as the 1930s, when a ship's program for the day began to resemble the minute-by-minute agenda of a holiday camp, the regency of Beef Wellington, *sauce béarnaise*, and Chicken Kiev was maintained at tables soon to be cleared for cherries jubilee and *crêpes Suzette*. In the 1970s, when the crunch came, caviar was the first to go or, at least, to appear on menus only on gala occasions. Nibbling their toast points, some people were led to hope that when the *France* was put up for sale she would be taken over by Iran, the one country in the world where oil and caviar were in supply great enough to bring back the good old days.

TOP: Dining with the Captain, whose table was usually larger and more centrally placed than this one.

MIDDLE: These diners on the *Cleveland*, 1909, of the Hamburg American Line are not among the 2,400 Third Class passengers that ship could carry.

BOTTOM: Dining-room stewards.

OPPOSITE: The dining room of the British-built *De Grasse*, which for two years after World War II was the only French passenger ship on the Atlantic.

TOP: *Crêpes Suzette.*

MIDDLE: *Pâté de foie gras.*

BOTTOM: The Purser's Table, a source of inside dope, as well as scuttlebutt.

OPPOSITE, TOP AND BOTTOM: To enter the 700-seat dining room of the *Ile de France* was to descend, under the *mal de tête* glare of high ceiling lights, into a vast mausoleum, faced with several shades of gray marble from the Pyrenees, additionally illuminated by a fountainlike spray of electrified Lalique. The furniture was of sycamore, the chairs upholstered in Veronese green woolen rep, the floor covered with highly polished india rubber.

As a phenomenon persisting into the 1930s, smoking rooms tended to be less the retreats of devotees of the weed than of men most comfortable in masculine company. When women in numbers began to smoke, propriety still decreed that they smoke elsewhere.

OPPOSITE: A lady joins the gentlemen in the warmth of the *Imperator*'s smoking room, where an "ingenious" ventilation system dissipated the odors of stale tobacco.

ABOVE, TOP: The smoking saloon of the *Leconte-de-Lisle*.

BOTTOM: That of the *Félix Roussel*.

ABOVE: The main saloon of Cunard's *Laconia* in the 1930s, populated by models almost convincing enough to be passengers.

OPPOSITE: Some of the same models in the *Laconia*'s emancipated smoking room. As traditionalists and modernists competed for control of the interior designs of the new *Queens* the Cunard Line was planning to build, decor of this sort came in for heavy satire. Since ships presented their national image, said a London paper, British ships should do away with the notion that England is exclusively populated by Beefeaters, Morris dancers, fox-hunting gentry, and bewhiskered characters mouthing proverbs in half-timbered alehouses. A columnist, taking up the cause, asked, Why not a *cobbled* gangplank? She didn't want to be reminded that she was "butting up the Channel in the mad March days," she said; she wanted acres of chintzy cheeriness, lounges and dining rooms as comfy and cozy as a coachhouse on the way to Hampshire—old gold, beige, *eau-de-Nil*, and lots and lots of flowery prints. Harrods, she said, had a marvelous range of tea roses. For a stunning reminder of our island heritage, she went on, why not make the First Class dining room a copy of the House of Commons, with the Speaker's Chair as the serving hatch?

OPPOSITE: The music room aboard the *Aurania*, circa 1938. This two-class ship (Cabin and Third) carried passengers (much like these models) from Southampton and Le Havre to Quebec City and Montreal.

The decor on liners crossing the North or South Atlantic usually reflected the ships' countries of origin, but long-distance liners serving the Orient were often decorated in the style of the countries to which they were going. In spite of many hands-across-the-sea gestures, North Atlantic ships resisted schizophrenic identities.

ABOVE, TOP: The *Félix Roussel*'s music room. On this ship the saloons, dining room, and music room were decorated in Khmer or Cham style reminiscent of Sambor Prei Kuk, or the temple of Angkor Wat.

BOTTOM: The music room of the *Cordillière*, a pre–World War I liner serving South America.

TOP: Auditoriums, some of them fully equipped theaters like this one on the *Normandie*, became conventional features in liners built during and after the 1930s. To make full use of them, particularly as cinemas, ship companies somewhat relaxed barriers between classes; on certain ships, First Class was seated in the orchestra, Tourist in the balcony (or vice versa); on others, each class was restricted to posted hours.

BOTTOM: In the *Normandie*'s *grand salon*, passengers respond, variously, to an entertainment.

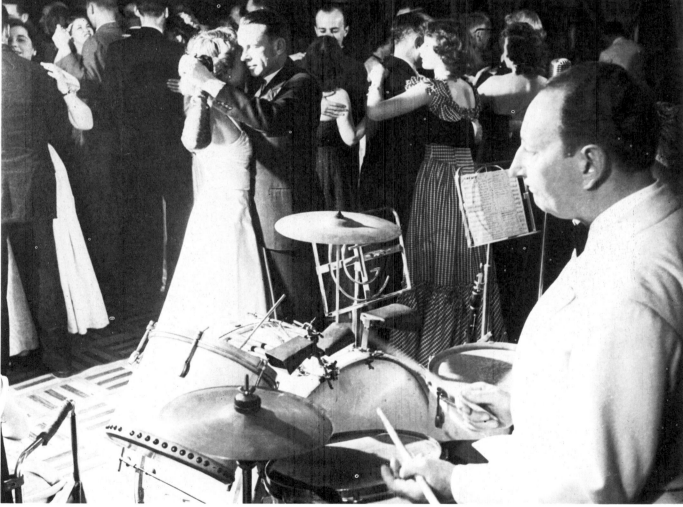

TOP: The Café de Paris of the *Ile de France*. This most famous of seagoing nightclubs brought together the intellectual elite of two continents and supplied them with silver dunce hats, glittery cardboard tiaras, and balls of cotton with which to pelt one another.

BOTTOM: The First Class lounge of the *Liberté* (turned into a ballroom by the removal of carpets) was sometimes open to invasion by persons from inferior regions.

ABOVE: *Matelot* headgear and *le jazz hot*.

OPPOSITE: Couples attempt to keep dancing without allowing the rubber balls placed between their foreheads to slip and so eliminate them from competition and the chance of a prize.

Landfall

The *Constitution* (sister ship and duplicate of the *Independence*) arriving off the Battery. Designed by Raymond Loewy, whose career began with fashion illustration and then moved on to industrial design, particularly in the field of transportation (the distinctive but short-lived Studebaker automobile was a creation of his), these ships opened a peculiarly American chapter in the annals of the last great liners. Crisp and brash, with high superstructures and clean lines, prefabricated bathrooms, and split-level dining rooms, and, in spite of their three classes, operated by staffs with easy democractic assumptions, they could have come from nowhere but the United States. As it turned out, they suited Americans almost exclusively. Floating Statlers, they had interiors distinguished by a sort of tasteful banality, no wasted space, and floods of natural light from midships aft. Congressmen and civil servants on home leave made up a good part of their clientele; and weather-conscious travelers, who could no longer bear summer voyages on the North Atlantic that seemed to skirt the coast of Iceland, liked the way they coasted through the Azores, then made working stops around the Mediterranean—Morocco, Spain, France—before sailing into the Bay of Naples. Their cantilevered sundecks above a swimming pool were later copied by Italian ships making the same run, and eventually by most ships engaged in cruising.

TOP: Arriving at Liverpool, the White Star liner *Britannic*.

BOTTOM: The *Vaterland* at Cuxhaven, in the estuary of the
Elbe.

TOP AND BOTTOM: The *Ile de France*, escorted and maneuvered toward her Hudson River dock.

PRECEDING PAGES: In late August 1950, the new French Line flagship *Liberté* comes to New York. Piloted up the Narrows flying the tricolor and heralded by publicity that gave her an aura of Bollinger Brut, *pâté de foie gras*, and let-'em-eat-cake snobbishness, she was a miracle of reclamation. Taken over by the United States Navy as a trooper at the time of the German occupation, she had made two voyages returning GIs to New York. Then, in 1946, she was awarded to France by the International Reparations Commission. That same year she was sent to Saint-Nazaire to receive fittings that might transform her from the sleek, fiercely modern Hanseatic racer that she was as the *Europa* in the twenties to a Parisian soubrette of the fifties. Lying at her refitting dock, she was ripped from her moorings by a wild gale off the Atlantic that sent her careening into the submerged hull of the old French Line flagship *Paris*. The collision tore a hole in her side so big that she filled at once and foundered. Dredged up from the ooze into which she had sunk, she was exhumed and glossed over with anything and everything Gallic that might disguise her Teutonic origins. Stuffed with needlepoint, Aubussons, and roseate draperies, the rehabilitated liner had much the feel of an older dispensation. Yet, for all the efforts put into her, she was still basically German; against the lambencies of scrolled gilt and curving tulipwood in *le grand salon* and *la salle à manger*, both Biedermeier and Bauhaus made tenacious claims.

TOP: The helicopter joins the fireboat in greeting the *Liberté*.

MIDDLE: Sliding up the North River.

BOTTOM: The demand for cheesecake persists.

OPPOSITE: The entry of the *Queen Mary* into New York in May 1936.

OPPOSITE: The *De Grasse* being tugged into mooring position.

ABOVE: The *Paris*, her hawsers caught by dock hands, approaches.

OPPOSITE, TOP: Disembarkation at night was unusual mainly because of the inconvenient working hours that would be demanded of customs officials and dockside personnel. But here the *Naldera*, arrived at Perth, Australia, one night in 1918, prepares to discharge passengers by arc light.

BOTTOM: Le Havre. After the luggage is moved onto the dock, confusion.

TOP: Passengers and luggage on the foredeck; tugboats about to cast off, warping to begin.

BOTTOM: Show horse and keeper about to be unloaded from the *De Grasse*.

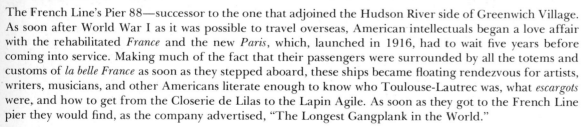

The French Line's Pier 88—successor to the one that adjoined the Hudson River side of Greenwich Village. As soon after World War I as it was possible to travel overseas, American intellectuals began a love affair with the rehabilitated *France* and the new *Paris*, which, launched in 1916, had to wait five years before coming into service. Making much of the fact that their passengers were surrounded by all the totems and customs of *la belle France* as soon as they stepped aboard, these ships became floating rendezvous for artists, writers, musicians, and other Americans literate enough to know who Toulouse-Lautrec was, what *escargots* were, and how to get from the Closerie de Lilas to the Lapin Agile. As soon as they got to the French Line pier they would find, as the company advertised, "The Longest Gangplank in the World."

ABOVE, TOP: Baggage porters.

BOTTOM: Transfer agents at the ready.

OPPOSITE: Having passed through customs inspection, each item of their luggage now ticked with chalk, passengers reach a final checkpoint.

228

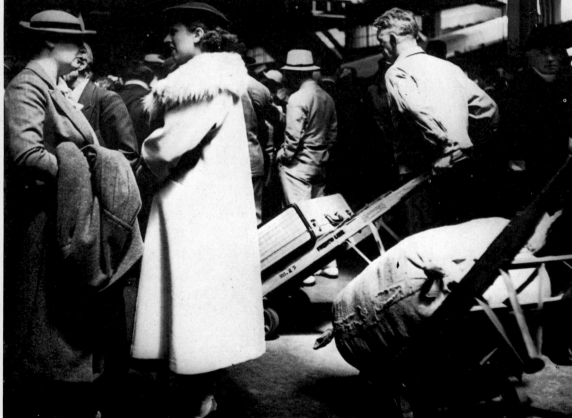

ABOVE, TOP: Customs inspectors and steamer trunks: hide-and-seek involving suits (labels removed) from Coco Chanel, Fortuny dresses, pajamas from Turnbull & Asser, *Ulysses* and *Tropic of Cancer*.

BOTTOM: "Be sure to give us a ring when you and George come to Schenectady."

OPPOSITE: Homecoming.

Emigrants admitted after Congress passed the Emergency Quota Act of 1921 were comparatively few. Commonly known as the Three Percent Act, this was a restrictive measure limiting immigration to that percentage of nationals of each country, based on the 1903 census. In the five years preceding World War I, emigrants had come to the United States at a rate of 700,000 every twelve months. When these numbers were drastically reduced, so were the profits of steamship companies. At their very lowest ebb, necessity generated the means by which most of the companies were tided over their worst period. Wearily contemplating half-empty ships and falling revenues, a number of passenger agents seem to have come upon the same idea all at once. Why not, they said, upgrade steerage to Third Class and soften the sound of it by calling it "Tourist Third" or "Tourist Cabin"? Why not pack students, teachers, and the good old American

middle class into ships catering just to them and send them racketing to Europe in fiestas of democratic *joie de vivre*? "Such a jolly idea," said one brochure, "coziness and friendliness more than compensate for any lack of the sumptuous." "Today," said another, "sub-debs, younger members of the smart set, college professors and students, men and women of the business world, definitely prefer to be debonair shipmates in the congenial atmosphere of Tourist Third Cabin when they travel to the edge of a new world and back again." It was not a new idea; it was simply one that had found its place and its good time. The waterways out of New York and Montreal were soon jumping with the beat of Dixieland bands as girls in cloche hats danced with boys in plus fours, or one another, on the open decks. Embarkations came to have the air of class reunions. Posed in formal tiers at the stern or on the steps leading to the sports deck, bow-lipped

(continued on following page)

231

(continued from preceding page)

girls in fur-trimmed coats, boys with slicked-down hair and in brass-buttoned blazers and flannel pants, solemnly squinted for the inevitable sailing-day photograph. The one in the front row center always had his or her head stuck through a life preserver, on which was printed the name of the ship.

The age of mass travel, of "tourism"—that phenomenon begun with a few nineteenth-century clergymen, lovers of old masters and Roman ruins, diary-keeping bluestockings, and a few families in the van of their possessions like sheiks in the desert—had moved into an entirely new dispensation. Now anyone who could scrape together eighty or ninety dollars for a round-trip steamship ticket and another few hundred dollars for a long summer in Europe was ready to join the great exodus.

The success of Tourist Third led to a category called Tourist Cabin, then to the gradual disappearance of Third Class, and finally to a whole new type of ship. This was the one-class liner, a floating democracy where no one looked down on anyone—neither socially nor from the elevation of a restricted deck. It was an idea that found most of its support in American patronage, and it threatened for a time to change permanently the whole character of ocean traffic.

One consequence of cheap and easy travel to Europe was a noticeable change in its general purpose. Before the 1920s, most Americans traveling abroad went to see the Botticellis in the Uffizi and the El Grecos in the Prado, to compare one Palladian villa with another, to wander moodily through the labyrinthine ruins of Pompeii, and to brave, like Daisy Miller, the mephitic dampness of the Colosseum by moonlight. To do this they had to put up with discomfort, diarrhea, and the inscrutable authority of an alien culture. Travel, as the prophet said, was a little bit of hell; yet to

most people the rewards of Europe were worth all the expense and trouble. But suddenly overseas travel lost its character as an adventure fraught with hazards and became an extended outing under the leadership, perhaps, of a professional guide from Atlanta or Minneapolis and, in any case, watched over by American Express. Instead of being regarded as the scene of new and challenging experience, Europe tended to become a place for fun—good and clean if that was your taste, or ooh-la-la if you had heard about those doughboys on leave in Paris and the mademoiselle from Armentières. In other words, Americans began to go to Europe on the pleasure principle—for the chance to drink when, where, and what they pleased, to live on a scale beyond anything they could imagine in Kansas City and Pittsburgh, to "have" the wealth of centuries without approaching it all with the holy expectations of pilgrims.

OPPOSITE: The view from Ellis Island.

ABOVE, TOP: Galician peasants newly arrived in Canada. Like New York and Boston, Montreal was a central point of entry for nearly a hundred years.

BOTTOM: Immigrants being admitted under the quota specified by the "Three Percent Act."

233

"*La Normandie!*"—the one resounding answer to a question posed by a patriot: "What palace, what triumphal way, what memorial have we built to perpetuate our civilization, as the cathedrals perpetuate that of the Middle Ages, the castles of the Loire that of the Renaissance, and Versailles that of the age of Louis XIV?"

Here the great ship sits at the Manhattan pier where in a few years, waterlogged and smoldering, she would roll over and die.

WARTIME INTERLUDES

For the shipping industry of the North Atlantic, World War I was a calamity of proportions not repeated in World War II. In the latter conflict, comparatively few ships were lost, most of these victims of aerial bombardment. But in World War I, when ships did not have the speed to outrun wide-ranging U-boats, and before they possessed the sophisticated means of detection that came with radar and sonar, the rate and amount of destruction were devastating. German undersea power, which, at first, threatened no more than decimation of the combined Allied merchant marine, was soon escalated to such a degree as to suggest obliteration.

Most ships lost to U-boats remain historically anonymous, including the largest and, potentially, most illustrious of all—the *Britannic*. Larger sister ship of the *Olympic* and immediate successor to the *Titanic*, this White Star liner, transformed into a floating hospital, was sunk in the Aegean before she could make even one of the transatlantic crossings for which she had been designed. While the *Britannic* and thousands of other ships that fell victim to German submarines were routinely counted as casualties of war, it was left to a Cunard liner to bring the reality of the U-boat menace dramatically into focus. The sinking of the *Lusitania* off the coast of Ireland twenty minutes after having been struck by a torpedo, and with the loss of 1,198 of her passengers and crew, including almost 100 Americans, was a crucial factor in hastening the entry of the United States into the war and thereby perhaps shortening it. Within three years, the cost to Germany of her military success at sea would be the expropriation of all of the surviving ships that once flew the Hohenzollern imperial standard. As reparation, or spoils of victory, the *Vaterland* was awarded to the United States and became the *Leviathan*; the *Imperator* and the *Bismark* went to Great Britian to become, respectively, the *Berengaria* and the *Majestic*.

The outbreak of World War II on September 3, 1939, apparently caught most of the great ships by surprise, some in danger at sea, some docked in alien and unfriendly ports, or home ports already targeted for destruction from the air. The skipers of those at sea at once acted on messages in code radioed to them from foreign offices; the captains of those docked at berths on either side of the Atlantic took directions from company headquarters, or made decisions on their own.

The old *Aquitania*, bound for England from New York, immediately went into the prescribed zigzag course of navigation that had so often outwitted submarines in World War I, and got to Southampton almost on schedule. The *De Grasse*, heading for Le Havre, made a U-turn midocean and raced for Halifax. The *Queen Mary*, declining to be pressed by terrestrial events or ruffled by contingency, kept on a serene and steady course for New York, but not without telling the Cunard office on Broad Street to have the new *Mauretania*, then docked at Pier 90, get the polite hell out of her way.

Newly arrived in the North River, the *Normandie* canceled her return voyage to France and stayed where she was, as did her aging sister ship, the *Ile de France*. The United States Lines' *America*, launched in Newport News only three days before the outbreak of hostilities, sat in her launching basin like a newly hatched chick, oblivious to the fact that there was a war on or that, under the name of *West Point*, her youth would be spent in the drab monochrome gray of a troop ship. The *Bremen* had arrived in New York on August 29—a most unpropitious date for a Nazi ship to be so far from home. Instead of turning around quickly and heading back to Germany loaded with late-summer tourists, she found herself thwarted by order of the United States Treasury Department. Impounded on a pretext allowing her to be searched keel to funnels, she provided the Attorney General with a chance to assure the city and the nation that he was on his toes. "There will be no repetition of the situation in 1917," he said, "when a democracy was unprepared to meet the espionage problem." Dark, except for her running lights, the *Bremen* was then allowed to slip away from the foot of West Forty-sixth Street, her band playing to empty decks, her hope of haven anywhere slim. Setting her course for a passage far north of established sea lanes, she stayed clear of the Allied ships and planes already stalking her and, for further protection, resorted to a naive but familiar *ruse de guerre*. Just as her predecessor the *Kronprinzessin Cecilie* had at the beginning of World War I tried to pass herself off as a Cunarder by having her funnels painted while she was at sea, and just as Cunard's *Lusitania* had once replaced the Union Jack with the Stars and Stripes, so the *Bremen* hoisted the hammer and sickle of the U.S.S.R. Keeping close to Arctic coastlines, her decks piled high with barrels of gasoline to be set ablaze should she be intercepted, she got to Murmansk in the remarkable time of seven days. Under the protection of her Russian hosts, she stayed in the Arctic only long enough to prepare for a clandestine passage south. Sailing from the mouth of one Norwegian fjord to another, she made it home to Bremerhaven, only to be attacked and set afire by British bombers at the very site of her launching. Good for nothing but scrap, she was then fed piecemeal to the munitions factories of the Ruhr. Melted down, the remains of the most stunning ship of an era were then spent like scattershot in theaters of war.

Trapped in the Adriatic, the beautiful Italian ships *Rex* and the *Conte di Savoia* could do nothing but await what fate and enemy bombers had in store. The *Conte* was the first to go. Sunk in shallow waters by the American Air Force, she was refloated two years later, but only to be towed to the breakers. Bombed and sunk by the Royal Air Force off Capodistria, the *Rex* likewise was pulled from coastal waters and sold for scrap.

Converted into troop carriers, nearly all of the remaining ships afloat were dispatched into waters they had never sailed, from Greenland to the Antipodes. Stripped to the bones of their tapestries and damasks, their murals covered with tarpaulin, their vast dining rooms transformed into mess halls, the British *Queens*, at times loaded to the gunwales with as many as 16,000 men and women, outran every U-boat dispatched to track them down and scuttle them and came through the war scarred only by the ubiquitous signature of a man named Kilroy.

While camouflage has always had its military role, the scientific application of chiaroscuro to ships in order to deceive enemy observers by distorting perspective was largely a development of World War I. Regarded by some historians—and by Pablo Picasso himself—as a by-product of Cubism, camouflage was particularly advanced by the French. Here, newly refitted for troop transport, the P&O liner *Ormonde* shows her dazzle-painted colors.

Le Paquebot La LORRAINE
de la Compagnie générale Translantique - BR - 2379

TOP: Converted into an armed merchant cruiser, the seventeen-year-old *La Lorraine* (her engines are the subject of the first illustration in this book) begins a successful military career. Among the twenty-nine ships the French Line would lose in the war, she would not be counted.

BOTTOM: 1917. The *France*, transformed and marked by the red crosses identifying hospital ships, arrives in Saigon.

TOP: The *Queen Mary*, painted drab gray, leaves port as a troop transport.

BOTTOM: The first World War I contingent of troops from Tasmania aboard the P&O Line's *Geelong* at Hobart.

The Cunard *Queens* as wartime transports shuttled nearly a million and a half troops between continents all the way from North America to Australia. Traveling zigzag, usually without escort, they depended on speed to thwart attack by German submarines.

When World War II broke out in September 1939, the *Elizabeth*, one year after she had been launched by the queen whose name she bore, was still being fitted out at a Clydeside berth. A sitting duck for German bombers, she was moved just as soon as she could be readied to put to sea under her own power, on February 26, 1940. In the hope of outwitting, and surprising with retaliatory gunfire, bombers sent to destroy her, the berth she vacated was at the next tide occupied by the battleship *Duke of York*—an instance, it was said, "of His Grace displacing Her Majesty." In the open

sea, almost empty, untried and unfinished, she was under a directive from Winston Churchill himself to get out of the British Isles and stay out, "just as long as this order is in force." A week later, under a broadcast barrage of propaganda meant to divert both German and British attention from her real plans, she began a crossing to New York. Five days and nineteen hours later, "like an empress incognito, gray-veiled for her desperate exploit," she turned up in the Narrows and was eased upstream to pier 90 where the *Queen Mary*, berthed next to the still-upright *Normandie*, was waiting for her. The *Elizabeth* would not take up the career she was meant to follow for another six years. Then, all the competition she had been designed to overshadow and engineered to outrun had disappeared.

On war-related assignments from Halifax to Singapore, the *Ile de France* entertained, and was entertained by, unusual company.

ABOVE: The *Normandie* in dry dock, to which she had access only after the *Paris* (visible in the background) had been dismasted and her three funnels had been removed.

OPPOSITE: April 18, 1939. The *Paris*, destroyed by fire only a few hours before a scheduled departure from Le Havre for New York. Fire brigades combated spreading flames for twenty-four hours, but the ship, thrown off keel by hundreds of thousands of tons of water poured into her by fireboats, suddenly subsided to port.

THE WAKE OF AN ERA

In the hot days of July 1956, it was a story no one expected to hear. But we followed it as portable radios on beaches, lakeside porches, and picnic grounds reported it, cheered the middle-of-the-night rescue mission of the *Ile de France*, and, next day on television, saw the lovely Italian liner roll over and disappear. Ships that should have passed in the night did not. Instead, the sleek bow of one had rammed into the broad side of the other like a swordfish skewering a dolphin. "I hear you were aboard the *Andrea Doria*," I said to my young neighbor a few days later. "Was it terrible?"

"*Ter-r-r*ible!" she said. "I lost my *skis*."

For those forty-four of her shipmates who had lost their lives, requiems were no less heartfelt. But the *Andrea Doria* casualty list was of minor account to a public familiar with photographs of plane-crash victims lined up in rows across the pages of their newspapers. The more impressive aspects of the collision and sinking were its reminders of human error in a circumstance where error on so broad a scale was thought to be no longer possible; and its revelation that old rules of the sea no longer obtained. Everyone was wrong—the Swedish mariners aboard the *Stockholm*, the Italian seamen aboard the doomed ship, a fact later tacitly acknowledged by an out-of-court settlement between the ship companies which had brought suit against one another, a fact soon forgotten. What lingered was the sorry story of what happened when the crew of the Swedish ship set about the rescue of those on the Italian. As the first

survivors were helped aboard, feelings of dismay and disgust all but overwhelmed many of the *Stockholm*'s crew and those passengers who had pitched in to help as best they might. Setting up tables of food, piling up blankets and first-aid equipment, they had quickly transformed the public rooms of the ship into a sort of Red Cross disaster encampment. But where were the victims, the frightened women and children they were prepared to receive and to comfort? Nowhere. The good samaritans found themselves handing out roast beef sandwiches and Scotch highballs to a hundred men in steward's jackets and a hundred others wearing the gray kapok life jackets issued only to crew members. This apparent reversal of an old tradition of the sea—from women and children first to deck hands and stewards first—was widely published in the following weeks; and its import generated both excoriation and justification. In the nineteenth century there would be no point at issue: Such behavior would have been declared blackguard and criminal. In the twentieth century, those who defended it, or merely countenanced it, took the position that any man has the right to save himself, especially if that man is an underpaid, overworked slave in the lower galleys of a floating pleasure palace. Except for those *Andrea Doria* passengers killed at the moment of impact, all were rescued. Had this not been the case, it seems likely that those crew members who were the first to quit their sinking ship would have become living reminders of an action no one could forgive.

A demarcation point in ocean transport was the Holland America Line's introduction of ships designed to provide Tourist Class passengers with all of the advantages once limited to those traveling First. The innovation effectively broke the class system of the sea lanes and might have worked wonders had not another introduction—jet aircraft that could cross the Atlantic in six hours—scattered at once any hope that people in numbers might choose to spend seven days crossing by ship.

The idea of a largely one-class liner was not new. What was new was the space allotted to Tourist Class passengers, the number of public rooms, the range of comforts approaching luxury. A traveler booking First on the *Ryndam* and *Maasdam* would find himself in a minority—one among 40 other passengers confined to a small upper deck while 800 others enjoyed the run of the ship. The ratio of First to Tourist on the *Statendam* and *Rotterdam* (ABOVE) was not so extreme as to make the well-heeled passenger on these ships feel underprivileged, yet it was still wide enough to diminish the Tourist passenger's feeling that he was getting less than the ship had to offer. Italian ships kept a minimal space for Third Class passengers, mostly students and Americans who once were emigrants. But by the time the *France* came into service, two classes were the rule, a rule that would soon be bent, if not broken, by the return to class distinction insisted upon

by the managers of Cunard's *Queen Elizabeth 2*. In effect, this last scheduled transatlantic liner offers, at least in dining arrangements, *four* classes, thus hearkening back to the early days of the century. But with a difference: The "fourth" class was once steerage and tin plates; not it is the penthouse suite and meals in the *à la carte* grille room.

ABOVE: American ships crossing the Atlantic in the nineteenth century were fast, extravagantly caparisoned, and quickly bankrupt. In the twentieth century they could have established a standard outstripping anything European carriers might put into the water. The difficulty was domestic and internal, the failure inevitable. When, on the *United States*, for instance, passengers could not summon their cabin stewards without first ringing for an assistant steward to transmit their requests, featherbedding had clearly gone to sea. And when, on one of the last American liners, it was estimated that overtime charges, kitchen to cabin, would bring the cost of a hamburger served at eleven in the evening to nearly one hundred times what the same hamburger would cost on land, the economic handwriting was on the bulkhead. Faced with a situation involving overtime pay and still another strike, the Italian Line gave up and turned the *Leonardo da Vinci* and its operation over to a maritime union. With no one ready or willing to give or accept orders in the chain of command essential to the running of a ship, the *Leonardo* soon became known for her bad housekeeping, sloppy service, and the dust and stale vomit that festooned her carpetings. Deserted by her old clients and proscribed by travel agents, she disappeared from the roster of illustrious Italian ships of which she was the last. "Unions have ruined both shipping and the theater," said a well-traveled playwright. "That's why there are no showboats any more."

ABOVE: Until the *United States* flew from her fantail a palpable length of cloth to tell the world she had won the Blue Ribbon—and, as it turned out, would keep it *in perpetuum*—that banner had for a hundred years been merely an idea. Applied to ocean speed records, the idea had emerged somewhere after the middle of the nineteenth century and, by the twentieth, was a widely recognized symbol without ever having become a sign. Coveted, the mythical pennant constantly changed hands between one country and another until 1909, when the *Mauretania* brought it to England for an astonishing twenty-two years. Then one day in July 1929, to the strains of "Deutschland über Alles," a new ship pulled away from Bremerhaven's Columbus Quay and set her bows westward. As all Germany listened in to daily ship-to-shore broadcasts, the *Bremen* crossed the Atlantic at a mere shade under 28 knots to wrest the Blue Ribbon from the

ruling figure of Britannia and her trident. Within the year, she had to surrender the legendary banner to her sister ship, the *Europa*. But the hegemony of German ocean greyhounds was brief. Fourteen months later the Canadian Pacific Lines' British-built *Empress of Britain* bested the *Bremen*'s fastest crossing time and kept the blue flag until, of all unforeseen developments, the Italian ship *Rex* raced from Spain's Tarifa Point to Ambrose Light four and a half days, and took it away.

This increasingly crowded contest led to a gesture by a member of the British Parliament, one Harold K. Hales, to bring the Blue Ribbon out of the air, so to speak, and give it weightier embodiment in the form of a trophy of silver 4 feet high and loaded with emblems and figurines drawn from maritime history. Soon after being awarded to the *Rex*, the Blue Ribbon Trophy was claimed by the *Normandie* with a speed that remained

unmatched until 1936, when the *Queen Mary*, cutting it by one hour and twenty minutes, was entitled to the prize but refused to claim it. "We do not recognize the Blue Ribbon Trophy," said the Cunard Line, somewhat sniffily. "We are only interested in having the liner officially designated as the fastest." Sixteen years later, the *United States* showed no such scruples, or hypocrisy. Breaking the Atlantic record both ways on her maiden voyage, she not only came into New York flying a blue pennant 40 feet long but took the trophy and put it in a glass box still on view to anyone interested in visiting what is left of the once mighty United States Lines.

ABOVE, TOP: Computer and control board. Like space center scientists, crewmen bring their ship to "Slow," "Dead Slow," "Standby," "Stop."

BOTTOM: The lone survivor. Except for Soviet liners sailing infrequently between Leningrad and Montreal, only the *Queen Elizabeth 2* maintains, between cruises, a schedule of Atlantic crossings on sea lanes pioneered by Samuel Cunard's paddle-wheelers less than 150 years ago.

For a fraction of her worth already cast off by those who owned her, the *Queen Mary* casts off under the eyes and valedictory arms of those who loved her.

That the *Great Eastern*, prodigy and masterpiece of the nineteenth century, and the *Queen Mary*, conceivably the most elegantly modeled, best engineered, and sea-wisest ship of the twentieth, should have ended their careers like monkeys with a cup or dancing bears on a chain is a fact that will not adorn the annals of capitalism. Anchored off Liverpool in 1888, the *Great Eastern*—product of the Age of Iron and the genius of Isambard Kingdom Brunel—bore on her hull the enormous lettering of a sign calling attention to a local dry-goods emporium. On her vast main deck, swings, rides, and food kiosks offered a carnival playground attracting Liverpudlians in droves until the novelty wore off and the fabulous iron ship, decades ahead of her time, was stripped piece by piece, mirrors, chandeliers, "Turkey" rugs, and pipe-fittings, and sold on the auction block.

The *Queen Mary*, consigned to a basin in Long Beach, California, more subtly endures the commercialism weighing her down. Yet, against all the desperate forms of exploitation with which she continues to be visited, she cannot help advertising the ingloriousness of her fate, or remind those to whom history is not, as Henry Ford believed, "bunk," that not long ago she was the apogee of man's old aspiration to master the roads of the sea.

The steamship era on the North Atlantic began on April 23, 1838, when two ships from England, the *Sirius* and the *Great Western*, paddled almost simultaneously into New York Harbor. That era ended midocean one hundred and thirty-nine years, five months, and two days later, at 2:20 A.M.

An excerpt from a journal:

September 25, 1967. The *Queen Elizabeth*, largest ship in the world, twenty-seven years old, is bound westward; at some point in the early morning she will meet and pass the *Queen Mary*, the next-largest ship in the world, thirty-one years old, bound east. This will be their final meeting, their last sight of one another, ever. For more than two decades they have been the proudest sisters on the ocean, deferential to one another, secure in the knowledge that they are the most celebrated things on water since rafts went floating down the Tigris and Euphrates.

Notices of this encounter have been broadcast and posted throughout the ship. But as usual at this hour (12:10 A.M.) most passengers have gone to bed, leaving only a few individuals strolling and dawdling on the promenade deck. Most of these have chosen to be alone; and they are a bit sheepish, a bit embarrassed, as though ashamed to be seen in the thrall of sentiment, even by others equally enthralled.

As the appointed moment draws near, they begin to disappear from the promenade deck, only to reappear in the darkness of the broad glassed-in observation area on boat deck forward. They stand apart from one another and do not speak, their eyes fixed on the visible horizon to the west as the vibration of the ship gives a slightly stroboscopic blur to everything they see. The mid-Atlantic sky is windless, a dome of hard stars; the ocean glows, an immense conjunction of inseparable water and air. Entranced, the late watchers try to pick out some dot of light that will not turn out to be a star. Hushed, the minutes pass. These ten or twelve of the faithful in their shadowy stances might be postulants on a Vermont hillside, waiting in their gowns for the end of the world. Then the light of certainty: Almost as if she were climbing the watery slopes of the globe, the oncoming *Queen* shows one wink at her topmost mast, then two.

Spotted, she grows quickly in size and brightness. In the dim silence of the enclosure there are mutters, the click of binoculars against plate glass, an almost reverential sense of breath withheld. On she comes, the *Mary*, with a swiftness that takes everyone by surprise: Together the great ships, more than 160,000 tons of steel, are closing the gap that separates them at a speed of nearly 60 miles an hour. Cutting the water deeply, pushing it aside in great crested arrowheads, they veer toward one another almost as if to embrace, and all the lights blaze out, scattering the dark. The huge funnels glow in their Cunard red, the basso-profundo horns belt out a sound that has the quality less of a salute than of one long mortal cry. Standing at attention on the starboard wing of his flying bridge, the *Elizabeth*'s captain doffs his hat; on the starboard wing of the *Mary*, her captain does the same. As though they had not walked and climbed there but had been somehow instantly transported to the topmost deck, the few passengers who have watched the *Mary* come out of the night now watch her go. All through the episode, mere minutes long, have come giggles and petulant whimpers from sequestered corners of the top deck. Indifferent to the moment, untouched by the claims of history, youngsters not yet born when the two *Queens* were the newest wonders of the world cling together in adolescent parodies of passion and do not bother even to look up. As the darkness closes over and the long wakes are joined, the sentimentalists stand for a while watching the ocean recover its seamless immensity. Then, one by one, like people dispersing downhill after a burial, they find their way to their cabins and close their doors.

SOME NOTABLE PASSENGER SHIPS

FRANCE Compagnie Générale Transatlantique, launched 1910. 1912: Le Havre–New York. 1914: auxiliary cruiser, troop transport, hospital ship. 1919: Le Havre–New York. 1932: decommissioned. 1934: sold for scrap.

Builders: Penhoët Shipyards, Saint-Nazaire. Gross tonnage: 23,769. Length: 690 feet; breadth: 75 feet. Turbines; 4-screw; 45,000 hp. Cruising speed: 24 knots. Crew: 500. Passengers: 535 First Class, 440 Second Class, 950 Third Class, 950 Steerage.

PARIS Compagnie Générale Transatlantique, launched 1916. 1921: Le Havre–New York. 1929: fittings destroyed by fire; after a five-month period of repair, Le Havre–New York. 1939: burned at Le Havre.

Builders: Penhoët Shipyards, Saint-Nazaire. Gross tonnage: 34,569. Length: 735 feet; breadth: 85 feet. Turbines; 4-screw, 46,000 hp. Cruising speed: 21 knots. Crew: 648. Passengers: 563 First Class, 560 Second Class, 1,092 Third Class.

DE GRASSE Compagnie Générale Transatlantique, launched 1924. Le Havre–New York. 1940-44: served as hotel for the Germans at Bordeaux, and later scuttled. 1945-47: refloated and refitted, served Le Havre–New York. 1953: sold to Canadian Pacific, rechristened *Empress of Australia*. 1956: sold to Sicula Oceanica, rechristened *Venezuela*. 1962: sold for scrap.

Builders: Cammell Laird & Co., Birkenhead. Gross tonnage: 17,559. Length: 552 feet; breadth: 71 feet. Geared turbines; 2-screw; 13,000 hp. Cruising speed: 16 knots. Passengers: 339 Cabin Class, 410 Third Class.

ILE DE FRANCE Compagnie Générale Transatlantique, launched 1926. 1927: Le Havre–New York. 1940: troopship. 1946: Cherbourg–New York. 1949: refitted, served Le Havre–New York. 1959: sold for scrap.

Builders: Penhoët Shipyards, Saint-Nazaire. Gross tonnage: 43,153. Length: 763 feet; breadth: 92 feet. Geared turbines; 4-screw; 60,000 hp. Cruising speed: 24 knots. Crew: 800. Passengers: 670 First Class, 408 Second Class, 508 Third Class.

NORMANDIE Compagnie Générale Transatlantique, launched 1932. 1935: Le Havre–New York, won the "Blue Ribbon." 1939: decommissioned at New York. 1941-42: requisitioned by U.S. Navy to be refitted as a troopship and rechristened *Lafayette*. Burned during refitting.

Builders: Penhoët Shipyards, Saint-Nazaire. Gross tonnage: 79,280. Length: 981 feet; breadth: 118 feet. Turbo-electric engines; 4-screw; 160,000 hp. Cruising speed: 30 knots. Crew: 1,345. Passengers: 848 First Class, 670 Tourist Class, 454 Third Class.

LIBERTÉ, formerly *Europa* Compagnie Générale Transatlantique, launched 1928 by Norddeutscher Lloyd. 1930: Bremerhaven–New York, won the "Blue Ribbon." 1946: allocated to France as part of reparations and rechristened *Liberté*. 1950: Le Havre–New York. 1961: sold for scrap.

Builders: Blohm & Voss, Hamburg. Gross tonnage: 51,839. Length: 890 feet; breadth: 102 feet. Geared Blohm & Voss turbines; 4-screw; 130,000 hp. Cruising speed: 27 knots. Crew: 970. Passengers: 555 First Class, 497 Cabin Class, 450 Tourist Class.

OLYMPIC   White Star Line, launched 1910. 1911: Southampton–New York. The largest liner until 1912-13. 1915: troopship. 1920: Southampton–New York. 1935: sold for scrap.

Builders: Harland & Wolff, Belfast. Gross tonnage: 45,324. Length: 852 feet; breadth: 92 feet. Two triple-expansion engines and one low-pressure turbine; 3-screw; 51,000 hp. Cruising speed: 23 knots. Crew: 860. Passengers: 1,054 First Class, 510 Second Class, 1,020 Third Class.

MAJESTIC, formerly *Bismarck*   White Star Line, launched 1914. 1919: allocated to Great Britain, purchased by White Star Line. 1922: rechristened *Majestic*, serving Southampton–New York, and came under the flag of Cunard–White Star Lines after the merger of the two companies. Largest liner until 1935. 1936: sold to Royal Navy as training ship. 1939: burned.

Builders: Blohm & Voss, Hamburg. Gross tonnage: 56,551. Length: 915 feet; breadth: 100 feet. Eight steam turbines; quadruple screw. Cruising speed: 24 knots.

MAURETANIA   Cunard Steam-Ship Company Limited, launched 1906. 1907: Liverpool–New York. Won the "Blue Ribbon," which it held for over 20 years; the largest liner at time of launching. 1915-19: troop and hospital ship. 1919: Southampton–New York. 1935: sold for scrap.

Builders: Swan Hunter and Wigham Richardson, Newcastle. Gross tonnage: 30,696. Length: 762 feet; breadth: 88 feet. Four Wallsend Slipway steam turbines; 4-screw; 78,000 hp. Cruising speed: 26 knots. Crew: 812. Passengers: 563 First Class, 464 Second Class, 1,338 Third Class.

AQUITANIA   Cunard Steam-Ship Company Limited, launched 1913. 1914: Liverpool–New York, auxiliary cruiser. 1915: troopship, later hospital ship. 1919: Southampton–New York. 1939: troopship. 1948: Southampton–Halifax. 1949: sold for scrap.

Builders: John Brown & Co., Clydebank. Gross tonnage: 45,647. Length: 868 feet; breadth: 97 feet. Parsons-Brown turbines; 4-screw; 62,000 hp. Cruising speed: 24 knots. Crew: 972. Passengers: 597 First Class, 614 Second Class, 2,052 Third Class.

QUEEN MARY   Cunard–White Star Line, launched 1934. 1936: Southampton–New York, won the "Blue Ribbon." 1940-46: troopship. 1947: refitted, serving Southampton–New York. 1967: sold to city of Long Beach, California, and turned into a marine museum and floating hotel.

Builders: John Brown & Co., Clydebank. Gross tonnage: 80,774. Length: 975 feet; breadth: 118 feet. Parsons geared turbines; 4-screw; 200,000 hp. Cruising speed: 30 knots. Crew: 1,101. Passengers: 776 First Class (Cabin Class), 500 Tourist Class, 579 Third Class.

QUEEN ELIZABETH   Cunard–White Star Line, launched 1938. 1941-46: transported 811,324 troops, prisoners, and wounded, traveling some 492,635 miles. 1946: Southampton–New York. 1970: sold to be used as a floating university in Hong Kong. 1972: burned.

Builders: John Brown & Co., Clydebank. Gross tonnage: 83,673. Length: 987 feet; breadth: 118 feet. Parsons geared turbines; 4-screw; 160,000 hp. Cruising speed: 31 knots. Crew: 1,318. Passengers: 850 First Class, 720 Cabin Class, 744 Tourist Class.

DEUTSCHLAND Hamburg–Amerika Line, launched 1900. Hamburg–New York, won the "Blue Ribbon." 1910-11: refitted as a cruiser and rechristened *Victoria-Luise*. 1914: auxiliary cruiser. 1921: rechristened *Hansa*, serving Hamburg–New York. 1925: sold for scrap.

    Builders: Vulkan, Stettin. Gross tonnage: 20,607. Length: 602 feet; breadth: 72 feet. Vulkan triple-expansion engines; 2-screw; 37,800 hp. Cruising speed: 16 knots. Crew: 536. Passengers: 180 First Class, 400 Second Class, 935 Third Class.

CLEVELAND Hamburg–Amerika Line, launched 1908. 1909: Hamburg–New York. 1914: decommissioned. 1919: allocated to United States. 1920: rechristened *King Alexander*, Piraeus–New York. 1923: bought by the United American Line and rechristened *Cleveland*, serving Hamburg–New York. 1933: scrapped.

    Builders: Schichan, Danzig. Gross tonnage: 16,971. Length: 588 feet; breadth: 65 feet. Quadruple-expansion engines; 2-screw; 11,000 hp. Cruising speed: 16 knots. Crew: 385. Passengers: 239 First Class, 224 Second Class, 2,391 Third Class.

IMPERATOR Hamburg–Amerika Line, launched 1912. 1913: Cuxhaven–New York. 1914: decommissioned at Hamburg. 1919-20: allocated to U.S.A. and sold to Great Britain. 1921: rechristened *Berengaria*, serving Liverpool–New York, under the Cunard Line's flag. 1938: sold for scrap.

    Builders: Vulkan, Hamburg. Gross tonnage: 51,969. Length: 883 feet; breadth: 98 feet. AEG Vulcan turbines; 4-screw; 74,000 hp. Cruising speed: 23 knots. Crew: 1,180. Passengers: 700 First Class, 600 Second Class, 1,000 Third Class, 1,800 Fourth Class.

VATERLAND Hamburg–Amerika Line, launched 1913. 1914: Hamburg–New York. 1917: decommissioned at New York, requisitioned by U.S.A., refitted as a troopship and rechristened *Leviathan*. 1923: New York–Southampton under the flag of United States Line. 1937: sold for scrap.

    Builders: Blohm & Voss, Hamburg. Gross tonnage: 54,282. Length: 907 feet; breadth: 100 feet. Parsons/Blohm & Voss turbines; 4-screw; 90,400 hp. Cruising speed: 24 knots. Crew: 1,234. Passengers: 752 First Class, 535 Second Class, 850 Third Class, 1,772 Steerage.

BISMARCK Hamburg–Amerika Line, launched 1914. 1919: ceded to England under the Treaty of Versailles. 1921-22: purchased by the White Star Line and rechristened *Majestic*, serving Southampton–New York. 1936: sold for scrap.

    Builders: Blohm & Voss, Hamburg. Gross tonnage: 56,551. Length: 915 feet; breadth: 100 feet. Parsons/Blohm & Voss turbines; 4-screw; 86,000 hp. Cruising speed: 23½ knots. Crew: 1,000. Passengers: 750 First Class, 545 Second Class, 850 Third Class.

BREMEN Norddeutscher Lloyd, launched 1928. 1929: Bremerhaven–New York, held the "Blue Ribbon." 1940: refitted to take part in the invasion of England. 1941: burned.

    Builders: A.G. Weser, Bremen. Gross tonnage: 51,656. Length: 898 feet; breadth: 101 feet. Weser geared turbines; 4-screw; 135,000 hp. Cruising speed: 28½ knots. Crew: 990. Passengers: 600 First Class, 500 Second Class, 300 Tourist Class, 600 Third Class.

CONTE GRANDE Lloyd Sabaudo, launched 1927. 1928: Genoa–New York. 1940: decommissioned at Santos. 1941: seized. 1942-46: sold to U.S.A. for use as troop transport. 1947: returned to Italy. 1949: Genoa–Buenos Aires. 1961: sold for scrap.
  Builders: Stabilimento Tecnico, Trieste. Gross tonnage: 25,661. Length: 624 feet; breadth: 78 feet. Geared turbines; 2-screw; 26,000 hp. Cruising speed: 21 knots. Crew: 532. Passengers: 578 First Class, 420 Second Class, 720 Third Class.

ANDREA DORIA Italia S.A.N., launched 1951. 1953: Genoa–New York. July, 1956: rammed and sunk by the *Stockholm*.
  Builders: Ansaldo, Sestri, Genoa. Gross tonnage: 29,082. Length: 656 feet; breadth: 90 feet. Parsons geared turbines; 2-screw; 50,000 hp. Cruising speed: 23 knots. Crew: 563. Passengers: 218 First Class, 320 Cabin Class, 703 Tourist Class.

LEVIATHAN, formerly *Vaterland* United States Line. 1922: refitted at Newport News by the Newport News Shipbuilding and Drydock Co. 1923: New York–Southampton. 1937: sold for scrap.
  Gross tonnage: 59,957. Length: 907 feet; breadth: 100 feet. Cruising speed: 27½ knots. Passengers: 970 First Class, 542 Second Class, 944 Third Class, 935 Fourth Class.

LUTETIA Compagnie Sud-Atlantique, launched 1913. 1913: Bordeaux–La Plata. 1914-18: troopship, auxiliary cruiser, naval hospital. 1920: Bordeaux–La Plata. 1931: decommissioned. 1937: sold for scrap.
  Builders: Atlantique Shipyards, Saint-Nazaire. Gross tonnage: 14,783. Length: 578 feet; breadth: 64 feet. Triple-expansion engines plus two low-pressure turbines; 4-screw; 26,000 hp. Cruising speed: 20 knots. Crew: 410. Passengers: 462 First Class, 130 Second Class, 90 Third Class, 450 Fourth Class.

MASSILIA Compagnie Sud-Atlantique, launched 1914. 1920: Bordeaux–La Plata. 1940: troopship, later decommissioned at Marseilles. 1944: scuttled by the German military.
  Builders: Méditerranée Shipyards, La Seyne. Gross tonnage: 15,363. Length: 577 feet; breadth: 64 feet. Triple-expansion engines plus two low-pressure turbines; 4-screw; 26,000 hp. Cruising speed: 20 knots. Crew: 410. Passengers: 464 First Class, 129 Second Class.

L'ATLANTIQUE Compagnie Sud-Atlantique, launched 1930. 1931: Bordeaux–Buenos Aires. 1933: caught fire, burned for two days and then abandoned to the salvage companies. 1936: sold for scrap.
  Builders: Penhoët Shipyards, Saint-Nazaire. Gross tonnage: 42,512. Length: 713 feet; breadth: 92 feet. Geared turbines; 4-screw; 50,000 hp. Cruising speed: 23 knots. Crew: 663. Passengers: 414 First Class, 158 Second Class, 584 Third Class.

FOUCAULD, formerly *Hoedic* Compagnie des Chargeurs Réunis, launched 1922. 1923: Le Havre–South America. 1928: capsized at Le Havre. 1929: refloated and refitted with fuel-oil boilers. 1930: rechristened *Foucauld*, serving Le Havre–West Africa. 1940: scuttled by German air force.

Builders: La Seyne Shipyards. Gross tonnage: 9,975. Length: 483 feet; breadth: 58 feet. Triple-expansion engine; 2-screw; 7,000 hp. Cruising speed: 14 knots. Crew: 190. Passengers: 320 First Class, 80 Second Class, 60 Third Class.

WINDSOR CASTLE Union Castle Line, launched 1921. 1922: Southampton–Cape Town. 1937: modifications made at Harland and Wolff Shipyards. 1939: troopship. 1943: sunk by the German Luftwaffe.

Builders: John Brown & Co., Clydebank. Gross tonnage: 18,967. Length: 632 feet; breadth: 75 feet. Geared turbines; 2-screw; 15,000 hp. Cruising speed: 18 knots. Crew: 440. Passengers: 235 First Class, 360 Second Class, 275 Third Class.

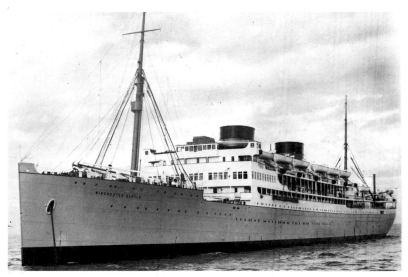

WINCHESTER CASTLE Union Castle Line, launched 1929. 1930: Southampton–Cape Town. 1939: modifications made at Harland and Wolff Shipyards. 1940: troopship. 1947: emigrant transport ship to South Africa. 1948: Southampton–Cape Town. 1960: scrapped.

Builders: Harland & Wolff, Belfast. Gross tonnage: 20,109. Length: 631 feet; breadth: 75 feet. Burmeister–Wain diesel engines; 2-screw; 15,000 hp. Cruising speed: 17 knots. Crew: 350. Passengers: 259 First Class, 243 Second Class, 254 Third Class.

STIRLING CASTLE Union Castle Line, launched 1935. Made its maiden voyage in 13 days, 9 hours, thereby beating the record held since 1893 by the *Scot*. 1936: Southampton–Cape Town. 1940: troopship. 1947: Southampton–Cape Town. 1966: sold for scrap.

Builders: Harland & Wolff, Belfast. Gross tonnage: 25,554. Length: 696 feet; breadth: 82 feet. Burmeister–Wain/H&W diesel engines; 2-screw; 24,000 hp. Cruising speed: 20 knots. Passengers: 245 First Class, 538 Tourist Class. Class.

ORAMA Orient Line, launched 1911, serving London–Brisbane. 1914: auxiliary cruiser. 1917: torpedoed.

Builders: John Brown & Co., Glasgow. Gross tonnage: 12,927. Length: 551 feet; breadth: 64 feet. Triple-expansion engines plus low-pressure turbines; 3-screw; 14,000 hp. Cruising speed: 18 knots. Passengers: 240 First Class, 210 Second Class, 630 Third Class.

ORMONDE Orient Line, begun 1913. 1917-19: troopship. 1919: London–Brisbane. 1940-46: troopship and auxiliary cruiser. 1947: emigrant transport ship to Australia. 1952: sold for scrap.

Builders: John Brown & Co., Glasgow. Gross tonnage: 14,853. Length: 580 feet; breadth: 67 feet. Geared turbines; 2-screw; 17,000 hp. Cruising speed: 18½ knots. Passengers: 278 First Class, 195 Second Class, 1,000 Third Class.

STRATHAVNER P & O Steam Navigation Company, launched 1931. London–Sydney. 1939: troopship. 1950: London–Brisbane. 1962: sold for scrap.

Builders: Vickers–Armstrongs, Barrow. Gross tonnage: 22,547. Length: 638 feet; breadth: 80 feet. Turbo-electric engines; 3-screw; 28,000 hp. Cruising speed: 17½ knots. Passengers: 500 First Class, 670 Tourist Class.

ORION Orient Line, launched 1935. London–Brisbane. 1939-46: transported some 175,000 prisoners and wounded, covering over 400,000 miles. 1946-47: London–Brisbane. 1960: used for emigrant transport following the merger of P & O and Orient Lines.

Builders: Vickers–Armstrongs, Barrow. Gross tonnage: 23,456. Length: 640 feet; breadth: 82 feet. Parsons geared turbines; 2-screw; 24,000 hp. Cruising speed: 21 knots. Crew: 466. Passengers: 486 First Class, 653 Tourist Class.

PAUL LECAT Messageries Maritimes, launched 1911. 1912: Marseilles–Shanghai–Yokohama. 1914: troopship. 1919: Marseilles–Shanghai–Yokohama. 1928: burned in dry dock.

Builders: Constructions Navales, La Ciotat. Gross tonnage: 12,989. Length: 510 feet; breadth: 61 feet. Quadruple-expansion engines; 2-screw; 11,000 hp. Cruising speed: 17 knots. Crew: 207. Passengers: 200 First Class, 184 Second Class, 109 Third Class, 826 Steerage.

CHAMPOLLION Messageries Maritimes, launched 1924. 1925: Marseilles–Alexandria–Beirut. 1939: requisitioned by French army. 1920: decommissioned at Algiers. 1942: troopship. 1946: returned to owner. 1951: Marseilles–Alexandria–Beirut. 1952: ran aground and broke in half.

Builders: Constructions Navales, La Ciotat. Gross tonnage: 12,262. Length: 508 feet; breadth: 62 feet. Triple-expansion engines; 2-screw; 10,000 hp. Cruising speed: 18 knots. Crew: 243. Passengers: 188 First Class, 135 Second Class, 128 Third Class.

FELIX ROUSSEL Messageries Maritimes, launched 1929. 1931: Marseilles–China and Japan. 1940: requisitioned by the Royal Navy as troopship. 1950: returned to owner. Marseilles–Hong Kong–Japan. 1955: sold to Arosa Sun Lines, serving Bremerhaven–Quebec. 1974: sold for scrap.

Builders: La Loire Workshop and Shipyard, Saint-Nazaire. Gross tonnage: 16,774. Length: 534 feet; breadth: 68 feet. Sulzer diesel engines; 2-screw; 11,000 hp. Cruising speed: 15 knots. Crew: 258. Passengers: 196 First Class, 110 Second Class, 90 Third Class, 1,502 Steerage.

LA MARSEILLAISE Messageries Maritimes, launched 1944 as *Maréchal Pétain*. 1949: Far East route. 1956: Marseilles–Piraeus–Alexandria–Beirut. 1957: sold to Transportadora International Co. and rechristened *Arosa Sky*. 1959: burned in the Antilles.

Builders: Constructions Navals, La Ciotat. Gross tonnage: 17,321. Length: 565 feet; breadth: 75 feet. 3 Sulzer diesel engines; 3-screw; 23,000 hp. Cruising speed: 20 knots. Crew: 100. Passengers: 279 First Class, 76 Second Class, 318 Steerage.

TITANIC White Star Line, launched 1911. Maiden voyage ended by collision with iceberg, April 14, 1912, with loss of 1,503 lives.

Builders: Harland & Wolff, Belfast. Gross tonnage: 46,329. Length: 852 feet; breadth: 92 feet. Two quadruple-expansion engines and one low-pressure steam turbine; triple screw. Cruising speed: 21 knots. Passengers: 1,054 First Class, 510 Second Class, 1,020 Third Class.

REX Italian Line, launched 1931. Genoa–New York. 1944: bombed and sunk by the Royal Air Force. 1947–48: refloated and scrapped.

Builders: Ansaldo, Sestri, Genoa. Gross tonnage: 51,062. Length: 833 feet; breadth: 97 feet. Quadruple-expansion engines; twin screw. Cruising speed: 28 knots. Crew: 810. Passengers: 400 First Class, 250 Second Class, 300 Tourist Class, 1,300 Third Class.

UNITED STATES United States Line Co., floated from graving dock, June 1951. New York–Le Havre–Southampton; also, in winters, to Bremerhaven. Now retired.

Builders: S.B. & D.D. Co., Newport News. Gross tonnage: 50,924. Length: 990 feet; breadth: 102 feet. Steam, D.R. geared engines; quadruple screw. Cruising speed: 33 knots. Crew: 1,068. Passengers: 888 First Class, 524 Cabin Class, 544 Tourist Class.

CONSTITUTION American Export Lines, launched 1950. New York–Genoa–Naples.

Builders: Bethlehem Steel Co., Quincy, Mass. Gross tonnage: 30,293. Length: 634 feet; breadth: 89 feet. Steam, D.R. geared engines; twin screw. Cruising speed: 22½ knots. Passengers: 484 First Class, 350 Cabin Class, 254 Tourist Class.

NIEUW AMSTERDAM Holland American Line, launched 1937. Rotterdam–New York until placed in cruise service; now retired.

Builders: Rotterdam Dry Dock Co. Gross tonnage: 36,982. Length: 759 feet; breadth: 88 feet. Steam, S.R. geared engines; twin screw. Cruising speed: 21½ knots. Passengers: in transatlantic service, adjustable from 574 First Class, 583 Tourist Class to 260 First, 973 Tourist; one class in cruising.

QUEEN ELIZABETH 2 Cunard Steam-Ship Company Limited, launched 1967. New York–Southampton; also extensive cruising.

Builders: John Brown (Clydebank) Ltd. Gross tonnage: 65,864. Length 963 feet; breadth: 105 feet. Cruising speed: 28½ knots. Crew: 906. Passengers: in transatlantic service, 707 First Class, 1064 Tourist Class; one class of 1,400 in cruising.

MICHELANGELO Italian Line, launched 1962. Genoa–New York; also in cruise service. Now sold to Middle Eastern interests.

Builders: Cantieri Riuniti dell'Adriatico, Trieste. Gross tonnage: 45,911. Length: 905 feet; breadth: 102 feet. Steam D.R. geared turbines; twin screw. Cruising speed: 25½ knots. Crew: 720. Passengers: 535 First Class, 550 Cabin Class, 690 Tourist Class.

LEONARDO DA VINCI Italian Line, launched 1958. Genoa–New York; later a cruise ship. Retired.

Builders: Ansaldo SpA, Genoa. Gross tonnage: 33,340. Length: 767 feet; breadth: 92 feet. Steam, D.R. geared turbines; twin screw. Cruising speed: 23 knots. Passengers: 413 First Class, 342 Cabin Class, 571 Tourist Class.

ROTTERDAM Holland America Line, launched 1958. Rotterdam–New York until placed in cruising service.

Builders: Rotterdam Dry Dock Co. Gross tonnage: 37,783. Length: 749 feet; breadth: 94 feet. Steam, D.R. geared turbines; twin screw. Cruising speed: 21 knots. Passengers: 647 First Class, 809 Tourist Class; one class of 730 in cruising.

STATENDAM Holland America Line, floated out of graving dock in June, 1956. Rotterdam–New York; also extensive cruising.

Builders: Wilton–Fijenoord, Schiedam. Gross tonnage: 24,294. Length: 643 feet; breadth: 81 feet. Steam, D.R. geared turbines; twin screw. Cruising speed: 19 knots. Passengers: 88 First Class, 868 Tourist Class; one class in cruising.

VISTAFJORD Norwegian America Line, launched 1973. Primarily used as a cruise ship.

Builders: Swan Hunter Shipbuilders, Ltd., Newcastle-on-Tyne. Gross tonnage: 25,000. Two diesel engines; twin screw. Cruising speed: 20 knots. Passengers: 660 in one class.

NAVARINO formerly Gripsholm Karageorgis Cruises, launched 1958. 1958: Swedish American Line cruise ship, also transatlantic Gothenburg–Copenhagen–New York, until sold to Greek interests.

Builders: Ansaldo, Sestri, Genoa. Gross tonnage: 23,216. Length: 631 feet; breadth: 82 feet. Gotaverken deisels; twin screw. Cruising speed: 18 knots. Passengers: 175 First Class, 682 Tourist Class; one class of 450 in cruising.

Index of Ship Names

Photo Credits

Archives Publiques du Canada: 104 B, 142 B, 145 B, 254 T & B.

Caisse des Monuments Historiques: 68 T.

Bildarchiv Preussicher Kulturbesitz: 78 (photo Hamann), 79 T (photo Hamann) 94 B, 200 M.

British Council: 47, 48 B, 248, 263 TL & BR.

Museum of Modern Art Collection, NYC: 114.

University of Liverpool (Cunard Line Archives): 24, 25, 41 B, 76 B, 87 T, 89, 146 B, 150 B, 151 B, 152 B, 158, 165, 172, 188 T, 196 B.

Compagnie des Chargeurs Réunis: 200 T, 265 TL.

Compagnie Générale Maritime, Compagnie Générale Transatlantique: 17, 18, 19, 21, 22, 23, 27, 29, 32, 34-5, 38 B, 39, 43, 48 T, 50, 69 B, 70 T, 71, 72, 73, 74, 75, 76, 77, 81, 82, 83 T, 86 B, 88, 90, 92, 95, 96, 98 T, 101, 102, 103, 106-7, 108, 109, 110, 111, 112, 113, 114 B, 116 B, 118 B. 119, 123, 125, 127, 128, 129, 131, 132, 133, 134, 135, 136, 137 B, 138, 139, 141, 148 T, 149, 150, 151 T, 153, 154, 155, 159, 171 T, 173, 176, 178 B, 179, 180, 181, 184 B, 185, 186, 187, 188, 189, 190 M, 191, 194, 195, 197, 198-9 (Studio Chevaujon), 201, 202, 203, 210, 211, 212, 213, 219, 220-1, 222 B, 224, 225, 226 B, 227, 228, 229, 230, 231, 234, 240, 244, 245, 261; Compagnie des Messageries Maritimes: 97, 99 B, 100, 102 T, 104 T, 190 T & B, 192, 205, 209, 265 M & B.

HAPAG Lloyd AG, Bremen: 42 T, 68 B, 98 B, 147, 166, 170 B, 193, 196 M, 204, 218, 262.

"Italia" Societa di Navigazione, Genoa: 264 T.

P & O Orient Line: 84, 85, 86 T, 87 T, 88 T, 99 T, 114, 116 T & M, 137 T, 146 T, 148 B, 152 T, 163 B, 164, 165, 176 T, 188 T, 200 B, 226 T, 239, 241 B, 265 B, 266 T.

Union Castle Line: 265.

Léon Coirier: 182-3.

Commandant G. Croisile: 222 T & M.

René Dazy: 32 B, 69 T.

B. Dunand: 40.

G. Feinstein: 265 TL.

Keystone: 41 T, 91.

L'Illustration: 33, 38 T, 42 B, 46, 49, 80, 83 B, 93, 105, 115, 124, 140, 157, 177, 178 T, 246, 247.

Baron Limnader de Nieuwenhove: 171 B, 184 T.

Photo Publicité Presse: 117.

Stewart Bayle, Ltd.: 20, 28, 36, 37, 44, 67, 94 T, 114, 116, 118 T, 130, 151 B, 156, 158, 163 T, 168, 169, 170 T, 206, 207, 208, 218 T, 223, 241 T, 242, 243, 263 T, 264, 266.

H. Roger Viollet: 87 B (photo Harlingue-Viollet), 142 T, 143, 232 (photo Harlingue-Viollet).

Peabody Museum: 31, 174 B, 175, 253, 267 TL, TR, ML, 268 TL, TR.

Cunard Steam-Ship Company, Limited: 30, 255 B, 267 BR.

Frank O. Braynard: 160.

National Archives: 251.

Holland America Cruises, Inc.: 252, 267 BL, 268 ML, MR.

Norwegian American Line: 268 BL.

Swedish Information Service: 268 BR.

Steamship Historical Society Collection, University of Baltimore Library: 267 MR.

(T = Top, M = Middle, B = Bottom, R = Right, L = Left)

The lines from "Arrival at Santos" by Elizabeth Bishop, originally in *Questions of Travel*, are reprinted from *Elizabeth Bishop: The Complete Poems* courtesy of Farrar, Straus & Giroux, Inc.

The lines from "Departure in the Dark" by C. Day Lewis, in *Word Over All*, are reprinted courtesy of Jonathan Cape Limited and Harper & Row, Inc.